Death in the Middle Ages

LIBRARY OF MEDIEVAL CIVILIZATION
EDITED BY JOAN EVANS AND
PROFESSOR CHRISTOPHER BROOKE

T.S.R. BOASE

Death in the Middle Ages

MORTALITY, JUDGMENT AND REMEMBRANCE

McGRAW-HILL BOOK COMPANY · NEW YORK

Contents

General Editor's Preface

In 1966 a large and handsome book was published by Messrs Thames and Hudson, with the title *The Flowering of the Middle Ages*. The text was provided by a team of scholars under the shrewd and skilful captaincy of Joan Evans, and could be read with pleasure and profit by all those who could afford to buy the book, and had an ample lectern on which to lay it. Word has come to the publishers that there are many who have smaller pockets and less ambitious furniture, who would like none the less to read its chapters as well as to admire the *Flowering*'s illustrations. They therefore asked me to join with Dr Evans in the pleasant task of converting the book into a series of small volumes, each incorporating a chapter of the original. The old chapters have been roused, stretched and shaken into a new and somewhat enlarged shape, have donned their old costume of pictures considerably increased, and now present themselves to the public for inspection. Their enlargement is designed to make them more self-contained, able to walk the world on their own; yet they remain a series none the less, and hope still to walk often in company with one another.

It is with great pleasure that I present to the public my colleagues' books in the Series. As I do so, I recall many kindnesses from many members of Thames and Hudson, and especially from the late Walter Neurath, who inspired the *Flowering*. I give thanks too, and above all, to Joan Evans, who first enlisted me in *Flowering* and has so readily welcomed and supported my collaboration in this revival and revision.

CHRISTOPHER BROOKE

Foreword
to the Original Edition

Fifty years ago history was mainly studied in school and university, and as a consequence by the educated reader, in terms of wars, political alliances and constitutional developments. Its base was properly in written documents, and even social history was not envisaged in other than documentary terms. Eight half-tone illustrations were enough for any historical work and most were not illustrated at all.

Now, at least for the general reader, all is changed. Schoolmasters attempt to give some visual background to their history lessons; occasionally even a professor of history may show a few slides. Professional historians and archivists rightly continue to study every facet of their subject in documented detail, but for most people 'history' has become a much more general matter, that provides them with a background to what they see and what they read. For them, at least, historians must so interpret the documents as to make them reveal the life of the past rather than its battles and its political machinations.

This change is due less to the professional historians themselves than to a change of view in the reading public: a change that can only be paralleled in the second half of the nineteenth century when trains and steamers made it easy to travel and everyone began to know their Europe. That time produced its Ruskin and its Viollet-le-Duc, its Lasteyrie and its Henry Adams; but we forget that Ruskin had to draw, or to engage others to draw for him, the things he wrote and talked about, and that Viollet-le-Duc was never able to reproduce a photograph.

In our own day a new wave of travel by car and plane has been accompanied by incredible developments in photography and in reproduction. Black and white photographs and half-tone blocks revolutionized the study of architecture and art at the end of the nineteenth century, and the great archaeological discoveries of the

7

day made the general public willing to accept an object or a building *pari passu* with a written document. In our own time colour photographs and colour plates have enriched these studies in a way that would have seemed miraculous to Ruskin.

Moreover, though education remains astonishingly bookish, our recreations have trained our eyes. An experienced and successful lecturer of 1900 said that a slide must remain on the screen for at least a minute to give the audience time to take it in. Now, the cinema screen and the television set have trained us in visual nimbleness, and we 'see' much more quickly. . . .

Somewhere about 1100 it seems as if Europe settled on an even keel. In England the Norman dynasty had established itself militarily and administratively. In France Philip I had established a rival kingdom, the Cluniac reform had revivified religious life, and the Crusades had started on their way. In Germany Henry IV was establishing the Empire on a firmer basis. In Italy Pope Gregory VII had lost his fight against the Emperor, but had gained new spiritual force for Rome. In Spain Alfonso VI of Castile had made Toledo the capital of Christian Spain, and the Cid had conquered Valencia. In the Eastern Empire the Comneni had suffered the inroads first of the Normans and then of the Crusaders; the weight of power was shifting westward. In Europe it is fair to say that a measure of stability had been achieved, in which the forces of feudalism, monasticism, scholastic philosophy and civic growth could work together to make the history of the Middle Ages.

To make that history more real to the ordinary reader is our purpose. The authors have not here published unknown documents, unknown monuments or unknown works of art, but have tried by the interpretation of what is known to make the Christian civilization of Europe in the Middle Ages more significant and more comprehensible to the readers of today. The keyword to our conception of history is civilization.

JOAN EVANS

Chapter One

Mortality

Death was a grim business in the Middle Ages. With no alleviation of pain, no dulling of the horrors of surgery, the *acerbitas mortis*, the bitterness of death, was very real. 'For two hours he lay as though unconscious and half dead; then I came and saw the father sweating in anguish, the pallor of his face flushed, his eyes filled with tears, the ball of his nostrils twitching, his lips bitten by his teeth. I said to a brother, "Of a truth the lord abbot now suffers much, for those changes in his members are signs of great pain." But he, gazing on me fondly – for he was so sweet – said, "Yes, my son, yes, yes, just as you say, I am greatly vexed by the agonies of this sickness; by the will of the Lord Jesus there will soon be an end to all this trouble."' *Note 1* It was to be for some two weeks in the Christmastide of 1166 that Ailred of Rievaulx lay in this final agony. These pious deathbeds were fortified by the acceptance of pain as an offering to God, but at the same time rendered more terrible in their details by the heroic desire for expiation. St Hugh of Lincoln, perspiring profusely in mortal fever, calling on God to hasten his rest, would still not throw off his cowl and hardly allowed his attendants to remove his hair shirt, though caked and hardened with sweat. Diagnosis was empirical and uncertain. Amaury of Jerusalem, against the advice of the Syrian doctors, ordered his Latin physicians to give him a purgative remedy when smitten by severe fever and dysentery. 'They administered medicine which produced the desired result easily seemed to give him some relief. But before he could take nourishment to strengthen his body which had been weakened by the violent remedy, the usual fever returned and he yielded to his fate.' Eastern medical skill, as William of Tyre implies in the above *Note 2* quotation, was in advance of Western, and was gradually penetrating the European techniques, which the more advanced Arabs 2 despised. Thabit, a Lebanese doctor, told Ousama ibn Munkidh how the Franks brought him a knight with an abscess in his leg, which he poulticed till it opened and began to heal. Then one of their own physicians intervened, saying, 'This man knows nothing about the treatment required', and asked the knight whether he preferred to live with one leg or die with two. The latter opted for life with one, and another knight was summoned with a sharp axe, who struck the leg a severe blow but failed to sever it. He dealt another blow, upon which the marrow of the leg burst out and the patient at once expired. 'I was looking on', said Thabit. A manuscript in Vienna of the second half of the fourteenth century, an Arabic treatise on surgery translated by Gerard of Cremona at Toledo in the twelfth century, is illustrated by grisly little pictures of an Arab doctor operating on his naked and unanaesthetized patients. Undoubtedly pain was a constant preoccupation from which we, whatever our new barbarities and dangers, are reassuringly relieved by medical progress.

Note 3

1

Expectation of life fell short of the psalmist's three score years and ten. Medieval records provide little reliable information, and men were often uncertain of the year of their own birth. When stated in legal business or tax returns, ages were clearly only approximate. Of the English kings who, between the Conquest and the accession

1 The most advanced medical treatises of the Middle Ages were those translated from the Arabic. One, translated by Gerard of Cremona in the twelfth century, was still in circulation two hundred years later, illustrated by surgical pictures (*left*) whose naive charm is at odds with their subject-matter

2 William of Sicily (*right*) is treated by an Arab doctor and an astrologer. Both treatments fail, however, and he dies. The manuscript is Italian, of about 1200

of the Tudors, died natural deaths, none reached the age of seventy. Five of them died in their sixties, with Henry I and Edward I, sixty-seven and sixty-eight respectively, the longest lived. Clerics probably outdistanced them, but here the dates of birth are generally uncertain. Jacques d'Euse was reputed to be seventy-two years old at his election to the papacy in 1316, so that at his death in 1334, defeating all expectations of a brief pontificate, he was ninety. Women then as now reached more advanced years, but their birth dates were not carefully chronicled. Eleanor of Aquitaine, however, was certainly past eighty when she died in 1204, after a life of stress, travel and activity little behind those of her male contemporaries. Such life-spans were for the vigorous and robust. The heavy toll of infantile mortality exercised a natural selection for the survival of the fittest.

Moreover, food easily turned bad in those unhygienic days and was a frequent cause of death, more real than the poisons often suspected at the time. The 'surfeit of lampreys' that precipitated Henry I's death was no doubt dangerously inedible. It was after eating stale fish that the notorious Fulk de Bréauté was found 'dead, black, stinking and intestate'.

Death in Battle

A sword stroke or spear thrust in battle might bring a speedier death, but even here the hacking blows of medieval warfare, where armour protected the more vital parts, were likely to cause wounds that were mutilating rather than fatal. Freeman's famous account of the death of Harold at Hastings, compiled though it is from writers of varying authority, gives a picture of defeat in battle that can be paralleled, if less eloquently, from many sources. 'At last another arrow, more charged with destiny than its fellows, went still more truly to its mark. Falling like a bolt from heaven, it pierced the King's right eye; he clutched convulsively at the weapon, he broke off the shaft, his axe dropped from his hand, and he sank in agony at the foot of the Standard. . . . But Harold, though disabled, still breathed; four knights rushed upon him and despatched him with various wounds. . . . One thrust pierced through the shield of the dying King and stabbed him in the breast; another assailant finished the work by striking off his head with his sword. But even this vengeance was not enough. A third pierced the dead body and scattered about the entrails; the fourth, coming, it would seem, too late for any more efficient share in the deed, cut off the King's leg as he lay dead.' The Bayeux Tapestry shows (though other interpretations of the scene are possible) Harold pierced by the arrow, and the mutilation of his body, while below Norman soldiers pillage the conquered dead. In this account of a battle of a much later date, that of Bannockburn, John Barbour, writing about 1375, describes how Robert the Bruce slew Sir Henry de Bohun:

Note 4
3

4

> And he, that in his sterapis stude,
> With ax that wes both hard and gude
> With so gret mayn raucht him a dynt,
> That nothir hat no helme mycht stynt,
> The hevy dusche that he him gave,
> That he the hed till harnys clave.
> The hand-ax-schaft ruschit in twa,
> And he doune till the erd gan ga
> All flatlyngis, for him falit mycht;
> This wes the first strak of the ficht.

Note 5

3 'Duke Harold is killed' – a detail from the Bayeux Tapestry (late eleventh century). Harold was said to have been killed by an arrow piercing his eye. His body was dismembered. At the bottom, Norman soldiers pillage other Saxon dead

4 The carnage of battle was not disguised in either art or literature. This fifteenth-century miniature of the Battle of Bannockburn parallels Barbour's poem quoted on p. 12

5 In this thirteenth-century manuscript Achilles and Hector are portrayed as contemporary knights on horseback, but the brutality of the killing is not less than in Homer

A fifteenth-century French manuscript shows the Battle of Hastings in the contemporary costumes of the artist's time but with much the same carnage as in the embroidery of four hundred years before. The brutality of warfare lives in many illuminations, whether they purport to represent the Battle of Gilboa or the death of Hector.   *5*

Sieges were followed by massacres and torture of the conquered   *6*
to make them reveal their hidden treasures; and when the victims were infidels, crusading piety gave a hideous sanction to the slaughter. 'For some of them, the easiest way, had their heads cut off; others were shot at with arrows and fell from the towers; some indeed were harshly tortured and were flaming with fire. In the streets and square, there were piles of heads and hands and feet. ... They rode in blood up to the knees and the bits of the horses by the just and wonderful judgments of God.' So wrote Raymond of   *Note 6*
Aguilers, chaplain of Count Raymond of Toulouse, about the capture of Jerusalem in 1099. Sometimes, without even the heat of battle, pillage and murder could be loosed on unhappy Jewish

15

6 Some of the most vivid representations of slaughter in medieval art are illustrations of Biblical or classical narratives. This scene, painted in the thirteenth century, represents the Massacre of the Witnesses in the Apocalypse

communities, whose ancestors had cried out for Christ's crucifixion, and whose present ably accumulated wealth tempted rapine.

And apart from the give and take of warfare there was the ferocity of justice, for treason and other crimes great or petty; and little clemency for captives in battle or for those who incurred tyrannical displeasure. An illustration to Froissart's *Chronicles* shows the execution of Aymerigot Marcel, the robber baron, whose only joy was 'to ride forth at adventure, when all the country trembled, for all was his going or coming', and now in the painting he kneels in his shirt, his hands bound, his eyes hooded, awaiting the sword stroke, while all round the scaffold windows are filled by a gay and interested crowd. The punishment for treason in England stipulated that the criminal should be hanged, but cut down still alive and disembowelled. Women, with an awful sense of seemliness, were burnt not mutilated. Elsewhere there were other ingenuities of flaying alive or pulling apart by horses.

16

7 The execution of Aymerigot Marcel, described in the text above: from a French fifteenth-century manuscript of Froissart's *Chronicles*

Chapter Two

The Last Judgment

Beyond the pangs of dissolution lay threats of greater torment and the overshadowing dread of the Last Judgment, that day of whose coming no man knew, when the blessed would be received into Paradise and the wicked pass to everlasting damnation.

The gradual formulation of detailed theories about the after-life is one of the obscurer processes of human imagination. The teaching of the Gospels was specific about spiritual survival, but imprecise about its nature. 'In my father's house there are many mansions' was a message full of liberal hopes and at the same time a warning against exact definition. It was the only occasion on which the translators of the Authorized Version used the word 'mansions'; in the New Oxford English Bible the word is downgraded to 'dwelling houses' as presumably more socially acceptable. It was inevitable, however, that heaven should become more particularized, and early there was confusion between the delights of Paradise regained, and a more abstract, Neoplatonic view of the Beatific Vision. The Book of Revelation provided a material concept of the Holy City which long influenced men's thoughts. The writings of the Pseudo-Dionysius, widely accepted as of Apostolic authority though not known before the early sixth century, brought, particularly in their ninth-century translation into Latin, some systematization into the angelic orders which surround the throne of God, and also stoutly defended symbolism, the attribution of shapes to that which is above shape, as a necessary concession to the weakness of mortal intellect. It was, the writer thought, a necessary cloak for profound mysteries, that could not be glimpsed by the vulgar. Men, however, yearned for more concrete assurances. When in the thirteenth century handbooks for the laity were produced, such as *La Lumière as Lais*, the blessed, it was stated, would enjoy all the uses of the *Note 7* senses, and experience beauties of sight, hearing, smell and touch. They would be in the full vigour of their age, for at the Resurrection

19

8 The Last Judgment, a detail from the west wall of Torcello Cathedral. Christ, in a mandorla, divides the saved from the damned who (bottom right) suffer in eternal flames while worms gnaw their skulls

of the Dead they would have the same age as that of Christ at his death, thirty-two years and three months, regardless of the age at which they died. Satisfactory visual responses were not easily found to such themes. The serried ranks of the saved provided less inventive stimulus than the sufferings of the damned. It was here that gradually the vision of the Garden of Paradise was elaborated. In the Eastern Church the Fall was visually linked with Redemption in the treatment of the Anastasis, the Resurrection, where Christ is shown releasing Adam from Limbo. In the West this was a much rarer subject. Christ's preaching 'unto the spirits in prison' was occasionally identified with the redemption of Adam and the Prophets, but almost certainly only when based on some Byzantine example. In the mosaic at Torcello, the Anastasis dominates the scenes of the Last Judgment, emphasizing the completion of a cycle in which sin has been defeated. In the West a vaguer, gentler conception ruled, the re-entry to the Garden, where the Tree of Knowledge was shown and where, as in Fra Angelico's version, the saints danced in circles on the grass, 'celestamente ballando', as Vasari puts it in his description of the painting.

The pains of Hell, unfortunately, lent themselves to more lurid and haunting concepts. In the sayings of Christ as handed down in the Gospels, particularly in that of St Matthew, everlasting punishment associated with eternal fire is clearly stated. These are phrases drawn from the Jewish tradition, symbolic statements of mysteries couched in the language of the time. Today they are one of the cruces of Biblical exegesis, but no Christian has ever been able lightly to disregard them. As early as the third century Origen, that most sympathetic and penetrating teacher, had questioned the theory of everlasting damnation, preferring some form (apocatastisis) of remedial punishment by which all men could in time be redeemed, but the Church as a whole, reinforced by the austere severity of St Augustine and anxious in this semi-pagan world to retain strong deterrents, rejected such glosses on the direct Biblical statements. The human mind has a morbid thirst for horrors, and gradually detailed torments became more and more specific. How these horrible images were elaborated and grew remains uncertain, but by the eleventh century they were receiving visual representation with a new relish, and no doubt something of their forbidding concreteness was due to the developing skill of artists in the

21

9 Another part of the Torcello mosaic shows Christ breaking down the doors of Hell, trampling on Satan and leading Adam and the Patriarchs of the Old Testament to salvation

rendering of natural forms, stimulating a search for new and arresting subjects in which their skills could be displayed.

10   In the *Liber Vitae* of New Minster, Winchester (*c.* 1016–20), there is a vivid realization of the theme of Judgment: in the centre a very youthful St Peter drives off with his keys a devil who tries to seize a soul; beside St Peter stands the recording angel with his book; beyond, a man and woman, pathetically clasping hands, are in the grip of a clawed devil; below is Hell's mouth, into which a devil propels struggling souls, while an angel locks the door upon them; above, St Peter flings open the gate of Paradise and beckons to a procession of the saved that stretches on to the opposite page, while within the New Jerusalem, shown as a walled city, the elect receive the Beatific Vision of Christ in Majesty. In the twelfth century this became a great and dominant theme of Western art. Here was a matter of deepest import to both craftsmen and onlookers, an unknowable but not unimaginable mystery, to which forms of lasting significance were being given. It was a public and general act of communication, such as is hardly found in contemporary art today.

8, 9, 26   The normal Byzantine rendering of the Last Judgment, as shown, for instance, in the mosaic on the west wall of Torcello (twelfth
9   century), begins at the top with Christ releasing Adam from Limbo;
8   in the second row is Christ in Majesty, between the Virgin and the Baptist, and seated rows of Apostles and the elect; below Christ's feet are burning wheels from which issues a fiery stream that flows down into Hell; in the third row is an empty throne on which lies the book of life with Adam and Eve kneeling before it, scenes that combine the vision of Daniel with the Apocalypse; in the fourth row are the angel with the scales, the Virgin in supplication, and on one side those who are saved, on the other the damned driven down into Hell. The West developed a more concrete visual formula, less involved with the Books of Daniel and Revelation, though the latter in illustrated Apocalypses had a long visual tradition of its own. The Resurrection of the Dead has much prominence. In the *Perikopenbuch* of Henry II at Munich (between 1002
11   and 1014), one page is devoted to the dead clambering, fully clad, out of their tombs, while four angels sound the last trump and at the corners the four winds, shown as horned heads, blow out a great
12   storm; on the opposite page angels lead the blessed up a flight of

22
10 Frontispiece of the *Liber Vitae*, *c.* 1016–20. Top: St Peter beckons the saved to Paradise. Centre: St Peter draws up one soul while a devil carries off two others. Bottom: an angel locks the door of Hell

11, 12 The Resurrection and Last Judgment, from the *Perikopenbuch* of Henry II, 1002–14. On the left, angels sound their trumpets and the dead rise from their graves. On the right, they are led up to Christ in Paradise or down to Hell

steps to Christ, seated between the Apostles; in the right-hand corner, as through a crevasse in the steps, the damned are dragged down into Hell where the devil lies chained. No torments are shown. It is still, as is to be expected in an Ottonian manuscript, some way from the final Western version.

13, 14   This can be seen fully developed in the tympanum at Conques, not securely dated but most probably of the 1130s, an early and masterly realization of the subject. Christ in Majesty is seated in an aureole; above, held by flying angels, is a great cross; on His right hand are the souls in the joys of Paradise, to His left is the mouth of Hell and the bottomless pit; below His feet the dead rise from their tombs and finally, on the lowest register, an angel separates the just

24

13 *Right*: Christ as Judge, from the tympanum of Conques (see overleaf). Beneath His feet the risen dead are divided into the saved and the damned

14 The complete Last Judgment tympanum of Conques is one of the most elaborate of Romanesque France, its message spelled out in long inscriptions taken from the Latin Vulgate

and unjust, the former being led towards a row of seated figures, framed in arches, the latter being thrust down into a second Hell's mouth. Here is a full programme of the after-life, dealing not only with the Last Judgment, but with the intermediate period before that great and terrible day. The wicked at death are thrust forthwith into Hell, still recognizable by worldly attributes: a knight who falls from his horse, a usurer with his bag hung about his neck. For them the resurrection of the body and the Judgment will only bring intensification of suffering. Below the tympanum runs in Latin the threatening warning: 'Sinners, if you do not mend your ways, know that a heavy judgment awaits you.' But for the righteous there is a period of rest and refreshment before the Day of the Lord will bring the full revelation of the Beatific Vision. Central among the seated figures in the colonnade is a venerable man with his arms round two smaller figures, who seem to hold flowers in their hands. He is the Patriarch Abraham.

26

15 'Here is Hell and the angel who closes that gate' reads the inscription
in old French over this fearful picture of Hell's mouth. It was painted
in a psalter for Winchester, probably between 1150 and 1160

In the obscure unknown beyond the grave, one certainty, as it seemed, was illuminated by the Gospel story of Dives and Lazarus in the sixteenth chapter of St Luke. 'And it came to pass that the beggar died, and that he was carried away by the angels into Abraham's bosom: and the rich man also died and was buried. And in Hades he lifted up his eyes, being in torments, and seeth Abraham afar off, and Lazarus in his bosom.' The Vulgate punctuates it even more forcibly, *et sepultus est in inferno*, 'and was buried in Hell'. It was a description that was early welcomed. Tertullian in his *Adversus Marcion*, written about 207, formulates the view that 'there is a spatial concept that may be called Abraham's bosom for receiving the souls of all peoples . . . which, though not celestial, is above the lower regions, to provide refreshment [*refrigerium*] to the souls of the just until the consummation of all things in the general resurrection.' The early sacramentaries in the prayers for the dead take up the same theme, praying that 'the soul of this your servant may be brought by the hands of your holy angels to the bosom of your friend the Patriarch Abraham and may be raised again on the last day of the great judgment'.

Byzantium used and approved the story. A tenth-century Gospel Book in Aachen Cathedral, a product of the German Ottonian school, that closely followed Byzantine models, has a page divided into two circles with (above) Abraham and Lazarus and (below) the rich man's table and Lazarus licked by dogs. A volume of the *Homilies* of St John Chrysostom shows, unusually, Dives on horseback holding his nose against the putrescence from Lazarus's sores: above is shown Antioch falling in ruins from an earthquake. The moral is clear: with death sudden and unexpected, men must think of their after-life. The Gospel Book of Henry III displays Dives in a richly decorated bed and below blackened in the flames of Hell. Abraham holding a soul in his bosom appears in the lowest range of the Torcello mosaic. In the twelfth century, Romanesque artists of the West found in these prototypes a congenial subject for their own carvings.

16   At Moissac (*c.* 1125–30) the scene of Dives' feast is shown with the dogs licking the sores of the dying Lazarus, while an angel carries off his soul, which is then seen wrapped in a fold of Abraham's cloak; on Abraham's right a seated, bearded figure points to a scroll; this is possibly another Patriarch, but the scroll suggests

16 This section of the porch at Moissac features the Dives and Lazarus
story at the top; in the arches underneath, Dives dies and devils carry
his soul to Hell

that it is St Luke, who gives Gospel authority to the scene depicted;
below, devils carry off the rich man's soul, as he dies recumbent on
an elaborate couch, mourned by his wife. His punishment in Hell
is then shown in gruesome detail. This is a direct transcript of the
parable which, if derived from some Byzantine source, has been
re-thought in Romanesque stylistic terms. At Lincoln, in the mid-

twelfth century, the scene has become more generalized, and Abraham, unfortunately a much damaged figure, now holds three souls in his lap while angels bring others to him. On the west front of Saint-Trophîme at Arles the Last Judgment is depicted on the jambs and lintels of the porch, with Christ in Majesty on the tympanum. Here angels bring souls to the three Patriarchs, Abraham, Isaac and Jacob, a rare interpretation: but Arles is full of unusual details, such as the door of Paradise closing in the face of the damned, who cover their eyes with their hands before this awful sight. At Autun, where the cathedral is dedicated to St Lazarus, there is some conflation of the two bearers of the name. On the tympanum of the north doorway, now destroyed, was depicted the resurrection of Lazarus of Bethany; on a still surviving capital of the doorway Lazarus the beggar, whose sores gave this combined saintliness efficacy against leprosy, is shown at the rich man's threshold and then in Abraham's bosom, averting his gaze from the pleading Dives. At Toulouse on a capital in Saint-Sernin, at Ávila in the church of S. Vicente, on a capital in the cloisters of Monreale, the same story is repeated, and a complete list of its occurrences would be a long one.

19

In illumination it is an equally popular subject. A Necrology of the abbey of Obermünster in Bavaria shows angels bringing souls to Abraham, while below him are the Tree of Life and the rivers of Paradise. The Psalter of St Louis, of the mid thirteenth century, shows the Patriarch holding souls, with Hell below him. Throughout western Europe it was a dominant theme, and the accepted symbol for the intermediate state of bliss to which the souls of the righteous are borne upon death. 'When a man dies', says the *Life of St Hugh of Lincoln*, 'he is led to the joy of Paradise or is snatched away to the horror of Tartarus, and there will he be; since between Abraham's bosom and Hell a great abyss is fixed.' 'That rest', wrote Aquinas, 'which is given men after death is called the bosom of Abraham.' In the Last Judgments of Laon, Saint-Denis, Chartres and Notre-Dame at Paris, Abraham and the souls are shown on a voussoir on the right hand of Christ; at Amiens Abraham, unusually, is standing, holding up three souls in the lap of his cloak; in the tympana themselves are the terrible events of the Last Day, and on the left-hand voussoirs the damned are hurled through a gaping mouth into the perpetual horrors of Hell. At Bamberg,

17

30

17 'Abraham's bosom' was commonly a metaphor for the resting-place of the good after death but before Judgment. This page is from the Psalter of St Louis, mid-thirteenth century

18 *Left:* souls in Abraham's bosom, from a portal of Bamberg Cathedral – i.e. not part of the tympanum, which represents the Judgment

19 *Top right:* part of the tympanum of Saint-Trophîme at Arles. The door of Paradise is closed in the face of the damned

20, 21 *Centre and below right:* two details from the thirteenth-century Judgment tympanum of Rheims Cathedral. The damned, including priests, kings and women of high rank, are dragged to the cauldron of Hell. Angels, their hands ritually covered, bring souls to Abraham

18 similarly, Abraham is a voussoir figure, while on the tympanum the elect rejoice in Paradise or howl in Hell with disconcertingly
21 similar grimaces. At Rheims, on the other hand, Abraham figures on the lowest band of the tympanum where there is a singularly beautiful representation of the angels approaching him, while on the opposite side the wicked, fully clad in their distinguishing robes,
20 are led to the cauldron of Hell. Above, the elect sit on one side, on the other naked souls are in torment; then comes the Resurrection of the Dead and above it the Virgin and St John kneel in intercession. This seems to be a reasoned statement to be read from the lowest row upwards. At death the elect are in repose (Abraham's bosom), the wicked are in Hell. At the Last Judgment these dispositions will not be wholly changed, but with restored bodies the elect will enter into a new phase of felicity, the damned of hopeless agony.

32

22, 23 At the Last Judgment the soul was weighed in the balance by St Michael. In both these thirteenth-century representations (*left*, from a Catalan altar frontal and *below* from a tympanum at Bourges) a devil tries in vain to pull down the scale in his favour

24 *Above:* on the lintel of a portal of Saint-Urbain of Troyes the dead rise from their graves. In the right-hand trefoil they are welcomed by angels, and in the left repose in Abraham's bosom, now a symbol of Paradise itself

At Bourges the Resurrection occupies the lintel. Above it is depicted the weighing of souls: on one side the elect, admitted by *23* St Peter, are entering an edicule where Abraham sits; on the other side souls are in torment. At a higher level, angels hover above the elect with crowns, the final reward of the blessed. Here the stages of salvation seem less clearly marked, and the intermediate nature of the place of 'solace' more indeterminate. The Bourges tympanum dates probably from about 1280 to 1290. Slightly later, the very beautiful tympanum of the west doorway at Saint-Urbain of *24* Troyes sets the Last Judgment in an elegant tracery scheme reminiscent of a window, an almost playful treatment which reduces the terrors of Hell to a very subordinate place in the pattern, and makes the seated Abraham serve as the main symbol of Paradise. Here, as at Bourges, it is no intermediate state, but follows on the Resurrection of the Dead, which occupies the lintel. At Rampillon

25 Resurrection was imagined in the most literal sense. At Rampillon (*left*) a man yawns as he wakes from the sleep of death

26 One of the problems about physical resurrection was: What happened to bodies which had been eaten and digested by animals? A detail of the Torcello mosaic (*right*) shows them being disgorged at the summons of an angel

25 (Seine-et-Marne) in the midst of a very realistic resurrection, where a man yawns sleepily as he emerges, Abraham, a highly classical figure has the souls playing round him as well as sitting on his knees.

These small naked figures pushing up their tombstones at the last trump were another field in which artists could heighten human expectations. If the bodily resurrection was, as the *Lumière as Lais* described it, in the perfected semblance of the age of thirty-two, there were still many problems about bodily reconstitution. The questioning disciple in the same *Lumière* was troubled about hair-cutting and nail-paring, and the teacher had to reassure him that

out of all decayed matter, God would make a new man, 'without
fault or excess, a hundred times more beautiful than the old'. The
Torcello mosaic deals with the Resurrection of the Dead in an
unusual manner, with no emptying of the graves, but instead, on
one side, angels force lions, tigers and a dragon-like griffon to dis- *26*
gorge scattered members, while, opposite, angels are similarly
employed with sea-monsters. It is a long, prosaic way from St
Paul's concept of a spiritual body. Official teaching soon discarded
such grisly fancies, but the popular mind clung to them as a
theological problem that they could both understand and visualize.

By the fourteenth century, however, views as to the after-life were losing some of the certainties of earlier times. In the twelfth century, whatever theories were expressed by theologians, the idea of Purgatory seems to have been little considered. The souls of the righteous were carried directly to Abraham's bosom or even, as on the page of a Boulogne manuscript showing the death of Abbot Lambert in 1125, into the presence of Christ. 'He surrendered his spotless spirit into the hands of his Father, and was at rest in Christ', wrote Walter Daniel of the death of Abbot Ailred of Rievaulx. In the scene of the martyrdom of Stephen on the west front of Saint-Trophîme at Arles an angel draws his soul up to God: 'and they stoned Stephen calling upon the Lord, and saying, "Lord Jesus, receive my spirit."' In the late twelfth-century roll of the *Life of St Guthlac* the Saint is shown lying dead while an angel carries his soul aloft; in a Shaftesbury psalter an angel stands with souls gathered in his arms, bringing them to Christ; on a tomb at Ely, possibly that of Bishop Nigel (1133–69), a great angel with spread wings holds the soul of the deceased in a napkin; on a Templar's tomb in Zamora two angels perform the same task; and it was a popular scene for the alterpieces and wooden frontals of medieval Spain. On the shutters of a retable painted about 1459 for the abbey church of Saint-Bertin at Saint-Omer, the painter (generally, though on inadequate grounds, thought to be Simon Marmion) showed the soul of St Bertin being carried by two angels, above the roof-top of the church, to God the Father seated in a halo of cherubim.

30

27

27
29

31

An accepted claim to this immediate transit to felicity was martyrdom for the faith. 'After this I beheld, and, lo, a great multitude, which no man could number, of all nations, and kindreds, and people, and tongues stood before the throne, and before the Lamb, clothed with white robes and with palms in their hands. . . . And one of the elders said unto me, These are they which came out of great tribulation and have washed their robes and made them white in the blood of the Lamb. Therefore are they before the throne of God, and serve him day and night in his temple: and he that sitteth on the throne shall dwell among them. They

39

27 St Michael brings a napkinful of souls to Christ – a schematic yet very tender painting from the Shaftesbury Psalter, mid-twelfth century

shall hunger no more, neither thirst any more; neither shall the sun light upon them, nor any heat. For the Lamb which is in the midst of the throne shall feed them, and shall lead them unto living fountains of waters, and God shall wipe away all tears from their

28, 29 *Left:* St Stephen's soul being carried up to Christ, from the church of Saint-Trophîme, Arles. *Right:* the soul of a bishop in the angel's hands, from his tomb in Ely Cathedral

30 *Right:* Abbot Lambert's soul, a small naked figure, is carried aloft to Christ by angels. In the semicircles are Almsgiving, Patience, the Virgin and St Bertin

eyes.' This famous passage of the Book of Revelation was constantly quoted, and was linked with the cult and invocation of saints. Those white-robed figures before the throne might intercede for common humanity, that had not the endurance for such triumphs. And, with the Crusades, a new element of familiarity modified the remoteness of these elect spirits. In one of the versions of Urban II's speech at Clermont, he is reported as assuring immediate remission of sins to all who die having taken the cross, 'whether on the road or the sea or fighting against the pagan'. This was accepted as meaning that crusading deaths were equivalent to martyrdom. Friends and relatives might now reach immediate bliss. On the First Crusade, while the forces of Robert of Normandy and Stephen of Blois were embarking at Brindisi, a ship overturned and some four hundred people were drowned. When, Fulcher of Chartres tells us, the bodies were washed up on the shore, it was found that the cross which they had worn on their garments was imprinted on their shoulder-blade, a sure sign that they had been
Note 8 received into 'the peace of eternal life'. An Italian abbot writing to St Bernard informed him that in a vision St John and St Paul had appeared to him and told him that those who had died on the First
Note 9 Crusade had now replaced the fallen angels. It is doubtful if St Bernard, with his subtlety and humility of thought, can have accepted this revelation, but it is characteristic of the fervour of the time, and the new pathways opened to instant salvation.

Such were the rewards and inspirations of pious self-sacrifice. The soul of the sinner, of whom Dives was the type, was snatched down to Hell by clawing demons, as shown on the terrifying slab
32 at York or on a capital at Vézelay, among other examples. There is in these representations a certain dramatic contrast between the pleasures of this life and the torments of the next. The powerful and wealthy were to have the reward of their arrogance and worldliness, the poor and patient were to find in the next world recompense for their miseries in this. Hugo Candidus of Peterborough, writing in the mid-twelfth century, put it in its crudest form: 'For the wicked in this life enjoy delight and tranquillity so that in this life they may reap the reward for any good, however small, they have done, but in the life to come they may find no rest. But the righteous shall endure in this world all their woes, so that they may rest in peace in the life hereafter.' Hugo, writing in the reign of

31 As late as 1480, in this panel from an altarpiece attributed to Simon Marmion, the journey of the soul to Christ was seen in the most literal terms. That of St Bertin is carried up above the roof of the abbey church dedicated to him at Saint-Omer

32 The imagery of Hell was rich and terrifying. This demon is from a twelfth-century capital at Vézelay

Stephen when it seemed God slept, was looking out on the troubled world around him from the devoted life of the monastery, but this was the theme also of innumerable sermons, particularly when the mendicant friars brought a new vigour to popular denunciation. 'At the day of Judgment', to quote but one example, from an English friar, Nicole Bozon, 'the simple folk will be exalted for their good deeds and the haughty abased for their pride. Then God will do as the mender of old clothes, who turns the lappet to the front, and what was uppermost downwards.'

Note 10

The *Summa Predecantium* of John Bromyard, a fourteenth-century compilation embodying earlier material, is lavish in its threats of damnation. These are particularly directed against the powerful and wealthy, the continuers of the Dives type, and there is an ever-increasing implication that those who fare well in this world will fare worse in the next. 'Their soul shall have, instead of palace and hall and chamber, the deep lake of hell, with those that go down into the depth thereof. In place of scented baths, their body shall have a narrow pit in the earth, and there they shall have a bath more foul than any bath of pitch and sulphur. In place of a soft couch, they shall have a bed more grievous and hard than all

44

the nails and spikes in the world. . . . Instead of wives, they shall have toads; instead of a great retinue and throng of followers, their body shall have a throng of worms and their soul a throng of demons. Instead of a large domain, it shall be an eternal prison house . . . instead of laughter, weeping; instead of gluttony and drunkenness, hunger and thirst without end; instead of gaming with dice and the like, grief; and in place of the torment which for a time they inflicted on others, they shall have eternal torment.' *33*

Note 11

This could be dangerous, revolutionary stuff, and it is not surprising that itinerant preachers were often associated with peasant risings; but more generally it may have had an opiate effect, redeeming present misery by hopes of future bliss. For either reason the death of Lazarus remained a popular tale which survived the Reformation and was, on the painted hangings that were the decoration of the poorer houses, familiar to Shakespeare's Falstaff whose recruits were 'as ragged as Lazarus in the painted cloth, where the glutton's dogs licked his sores'. In the moving homily *The Fear of Death*, possibly written by Cranmer, and directed under Elizabeth to be read in the churches, the story of Lazarus was recounted. 'So unto this place bodily death sendeth all them that in this world have their joy and felicity, all them that in this world be unfaithful unto God and uncharitable unto their neighbours, so dying without repentance and hope of God's mercy.'

Note 12

33 'Instead of wives, they shall have toads; instead of a great retinue and throng of followers, their body shall have a throng of worms.' The prophecy of John Bromyard is given hideous illustration in the tomb of François de Sarra (*c.* 1400)

34

The pious went to Abraham's bosom, the wicked to the cauldron of Hell. But then as now the ordinary man was neither outstandingly virtuous nor thoroughly bad; the Last Judgment must to many have appeared a very real weighing of souls, the outcome of which was no foregone conclusion. If the elect and the damned each had their place of waiting for that Judgment, what happened to those in between these states? To the early Fathers the millennium was not long distant, and the mediate period therefore one of short duration, whose nature they were content to leave imprecise. With St Augustine the doctrine of purifying and expiatory pain between death and judgment was established. Whether all pass through Purgatory or only those who have inadequately atoned on earth remained something of an open question. Augustine himself wrote of his dead friend Nebridius: 'Now he lives in Abraham's bosom. Whatsoever that state be, which is signified by that bosom, there lives Nebridius my sweet friend . . . for what other place is there for such a soul?' Writing in the early twelfth century, Honorius of Autun held that purgation could, wholly or partially, be accomplished in this world by self-inflicted fasts and penances, by loss of worldly goods, by want of food and clothing or by the bitterness of death itself. After death there would be purgation by the heat of fire or the rigour of cold or by some other punishments, the least of which would be greater than anything imaginable in this life, but in these purifying torments angels and saints would appear to those suffering them and there would be hope of salvation.

St Bernard is more explicit: there are three regions, Hell where there is no redemption, Purgatory where there is hope, and Paradise where there is the Beatific Vision. To the middle path of Purgatory the generality of mankind is committed by its humanity: 'I will go there and I will see the great vision, how the Father leaves his sons in the hand of the tormentor that they may be glorified, not to kill, but to purge'. This was a doctrine that received steady confirmation from writers such as Vincent of Beauvais and St Thomas Aquinas, and in 1274 at the Council of Lyons, where Pope Gregory X was striving, in the interests of the crusading kingdom, to achieve some unity with the Eastern Church, Purgatory and the efficacy of prayers for the dead were included in an agreed

46

34 'And they shall see the Son of Man coming in a cloud with power and great glory.' *Right:* a miniature illustrating the Second Coming

profession of faith. The extent, however, to which penance on earth and blamelessness of life could, as it were, by-pass Purgatory and bring the soul at once to bliss remained something of an open question. In 1331 Pope John XXII alarmed theological circles by a series of sermons in which he preached that none, however worthy, could enjoy the Beatific Vision before the Last Judgment. This was held to threaten the validity of intercession by the saints, and was formally contradicted by his successor, Benedict XII, in 1336. By now the doctrine of the Treasury of Merits, the infinite merits of Christ and the accumulated virtues of saints and martyrs, whose resources could be administered by the Church, was widely held as a means of salvation, and anything that questioned its efficacy in reducing the period of purgation roused much popular resistance. Indulgences, by which part of the temporal penance, due to sin even after repentance and absolution, was remitted, could be earned by joining a crusade, making a pilgrimage to a particular shrine, or building a church; eventually they could simply be bought. As penance on earth might lessen Purgatorial suffering, these substitute penances were matters of great moment, and popular shrines or papal agents had a vested interest in them. The high imagination of Dante could invest Purgatory with deep spiritual significance. Mystics such as Juliana of Norwich could desire 'full sight of Hell and Purgatory', and meditate upon 'the medicines by which the soul is saved'; but more generally it was torment rather than spiritual progress that was emphasized. Lurid legends circulated:

35 King Dagobert rescued from demons by St Denis, St Maurice and St Martin: a hermit's vision embodied in the monument erected by Louis IX in the early thirteenth century

36 The whole west wall of Chaldon church, Surrey, is painted with
this fresco of souls falling from a ladder into the clutches of frightful
demons

Peter of Branham tells how a certain chaplain walking in the
countryside suddenly met his dead father riding with his concubine,
who carried her child that had died without baptism. The father
had confessed his sins and repented, else he would now have been in
Hell, whereas he was in Purgatory, where there was the consola-
tion of hope; *in inferno nulla est consolatio*. The chaplain then saw a
vision of Purgatory: flames and sulphur on one side, frost and
terrible cold on the other, filled with figures whose various garments and states of nudity distinguished the various sins and degrees
of repentance before death. Outside Italy, where Dante's *Divina*   Note 13
Commedia found some visual realizations, there was, however,
little attempt to represent Purgatory in painting or sculpture.
Imagination seemed to have been exhausted by the effort of embodying Hell. In the church of Chaldon in Surrey a fresco, of about   36
1200, represents a ladder with souls upon it, some climbing, some
falling from it, which may have some Purgatorial implications.

On the splendid monument erected in Saint-Denis by Louis IX
to King Dagobert, a relief behind the recumbent effigy retails a
legend, the meaning of which is explained by Guillaume de Nangis,
who knew well this carving in his own monastery. St Denis on the
death of Dagobert commanded a hermit, John, to pray for the
King's soul; in a vision the hermit saw the soul of Dagobert in a
boat tormented by demons, but St Denis, St Maurice and St Martin
appeared and rescued him, carrying him aloft in a cloth to Abraham's bosom – or so says Guillaume though the figure in the very
apex of the arch might well be God the Father. This is a clear state-

35
Note 14

37 'On the right side will be Purgatory' runs the contract for Enguerrand
Quarton's altarpiece at Avignon. 'On the left side will be Hell.' The
landscapes above them represent Rome (though Moses and the burning
bush is included) and Jerusalem with the Temple

ment of the validity of the invocation of saints, but it was commissioned by a king, himself a saint, and cannot be taken as representative of widespread opinion. Another striking illustration of the doctrine comes appropriately from Avignon, securely dated by a detailed contract to 1453, the painting of the Coronation of the Virgin by Enguerrand Quarton. In the centre, the Trinity crown the Virgin, their wide-spreading cloaks forming a great circular pattern. On either side, much smaller in scale, are groups of the elect. On a hill below, between very generalized representations of Rome and Jerusalem, a monk kneels before the crucifix. At the very foot an angel releases souls from the flames of Purgatory, and a devil drives others into the torments of Hell. In 1439, at the Council of Florence, Purgatory had received further affirmation in the discussions with the Orthodox Church, and this Avignon altarpiece may be taken as a visual statement of the revived doctrinal interest. In keeping with this new emphasis is the gradual

38 Horrors multiplied in the elaborate paintings of the Last Judgment characteristic of the later Middle Ages. This detail (*left*) is from that by Stefan Lochner, of about 1430

39 The figure of Abraham eventually merged with that of God the Father, who is probably represented (*right*) at the top of the Percy tomb in Beverley Minster

disappearance in visual art of the figure of Abraham. On the topmost pinnacle of the tomb of Lady Eleanor Percy (d. 1328) at Beverley a bearded figure holds a little naked soul kneeling in prayer in the lap of his garment, and this is more likely the figure of God than the intermediate resting-place in the Patriarch's bosom. In the great fifteenth-century representations of the Last Day, such as Stefan Lochner's wonderful mingling of tenderness and brutality, Abraham seldom appears. He retained, however, his place in the liturgy and was long a familiar name in popular speech. When in Shakespeare's *Richard II* Bolingbroke hears the news of Thomas Mowbray's death, he says, with a certain flippancy, as though using an outdated formula: 39

38

> Sweet peace conduct his sweet soul to the bosom
> Of good old Abraham.

Even more clearly cynical is Richard III's comment on the murdered princes, 'The sons of Edward sleep in Abraham's bosom.' There is more feeling, more survival of traditional belief, despite some verbal confusion, in mine hostess's account of Falstaff's end: 'Nay, sure, he's not in hell, he's in Arthur's bosom, if ever man went to Arthur's bosom.'

53

40, 41 From the fourteenth century onwards, popular ideas of Hell, Purgatory and Paradise were largely conditioned by Dante's vivid narrative of the *Divina Commedia*. *Above:* a drawing by Botticelli illustrating Canto XXIX of the *Inferno*, the circle of the Falsifiers, stricken with horrible diseases. *Right:* detail from the fresco commemorating Dante in Florence Cathedral. On the left the path descends to Hell; on on the right, by steep steps, it ascends through Purgatory to Heaven

40–42   Italy was another matter. The *Divina Commedia* had rapidly, at least in educated circles, become an authoritative statement about the after-life, with both a philosophy and a cosmography as guides

41   to its nature. The seven terraces of Purgatory, with the graded ascents between them, lead to the terrestrial Paradise, the lost Eden:

> Those who in ancient times have feigned in song
> The Age of Gold and its felicity,
> Dreamed of this place perhaps upon Parnassus.

From there, Dante passes to the spheres of Heaven and

> things beheld, which to repeat
> Nor knows, nor can, who from above returns

OELVM CECINIT MEDIVMQVE IMVMQVE TRIBVNAL   LVSTRAVITQVE ANIMO CVNCTA PO

> Because in drawing near to its desire
> Our intellect ingulphs itself so far,
> That after it the memory cannot go.

In the great final cantos of the *Paradiso*, human speculation about the vision of God reaches its highest expression. It is a Heaven populated with saints, semicircles bathed in light, that were to be approached by no visual realization till Raphael painted the *Disputa*. But the final consummation is abstract and mathematical:

> As the geometrician, who endeavours
> To square the circle, and discovers not,
> By taking thought, the principle he wants,
> Even such was I.

With his amazing imaginative power Dante finds terms more closely akin to our own age, with its accustomed scientific formulas and non-representational art, than they can have been to trecento Italy:

> I saw that in its depth, far down is lying
> Bound up with love together in one volume,
> What through the universe in leaves is scattered,
> Substance, and accident, and their operations,
> All interfused together in such wise
> That what I speak of is one simple light.
> The universal fashion of this knot
> Methinks I saw, since more abundantly
> In saying this I feel that I rejoice.

This is far removed from the anthropomorphism of Romanesque or Gothic art. Never before or since has the ineffable been more nearly defined.

The *Inferno* is less raised above its period. Compassion battles with the austerity of justice, and human frailty finds some of its greatest poetic understanding; but the torments of Hell, though now more closely fitted to the offence, have the medieval tradition not far behind them. Nardo di Cione's fresco in Sta Maria Novella in Florence follows the scheme of Dante's circles with full appreciation of its horrors. In the Bolognini chapel in S. Petronio in Bologna, Giovanni da Modena's *Last Judgment* uses Dante's configuration, but vigorously carries out the instructions in the will of the donor that the torments should be made as horrible as possible.

42

42 Dante's *Inferno*, with its nine circles of torment, is depicted in detail in Nardo di Cione's fresco in Sta Maria Novella, Florence

Chapter Three

Prayers for the Dead

With Purgatory a more accepted concept, prayers for the dead received proportionately more urgency.

In the twelfth century grants to churches and abbeys had in mind prayers for the living as much as prayers for the departed. When the kings and queens of England began to endow the community at Fontevrault, their donations had in view the welfare of their families and kingdom: they were grants for 'the salvation of me and mine', 'for the peace and safety of my kingdom'. But as Fontevrault became recognized as the burial-place of the royal house, the emphasis changed. Eleanor of Aquitaine in 1199, *44* assigning a considerable grant to the convent, where she herself so often resided in her widowhood, does so 'for the souls of King Henry, her son King Henry, of goodly memory and of that mighty man King Richard'. Here, in this spiritual centre of the strong, *Note 15* determined, ruthless Angevin family, a treasure of perpetual prayer was to be laid up. At Westminster in 1220, those who contributed to the building of the Lady Chapel were promised thirteen Masses for the living, at the main festivals of the Church, but for the dead twenty Masses each week.

At Fontevrault and Westminster the community for a time could carry out these services without any special appointments for the function. But as the demands of pious benefactors became more exacting, and the realization of Purgatorial pains ever more vivid, order had to be taken for the carrying out of these obligations. When Louis IX of France was dying on the hillside above Carthage, he gave to his son a letter setting out his own theory of good rule, and at the end he wrote: 'Lastly, sweet son, cause Masses to be chanted and prayers offered up for my soul throughout thy kingdom.' This was a precedent with the weight of sanctity behind *Note 16* it. In England a great affection gave the new impetus. When Eleanor of Castile died, her husband Edward I was heart-broken

59

43 The mourner: Warwick the Kingmaker, a small figure on the tomb of his father-in-law in the Beauchamp Chapel, Warwick

for her 'whom living I have dearly cherished and whom dead I shall not cease to love'. As the body was brought from Hardby in Lincolnshire to Westminster, memorial crosses were set up at each stopping-place, following perhaps an example that had been given in France when St Louis's body was carried through France. At Hardby, Edington, Blackfriars in London, and Westminster, perpetual endowments for Masses were set up, and priests were salaried and appointed to celebrate them. No less than twenty-two manors were given by Edward to Westminster. Day and night two large wax candles were kept burning by Eleanor's tomb, and on feast-days thirty were lit round it. And so it continued until the Reformation brought other modes. The tomb itself is in bronze and was the work of William Torel, who had also been responsible for the effigy of Edward's father, Henry III. Eleanor lies with her head on patterned cushions, her eyes open, her long hair framing her face, her garments falling in straight folds. One arm is folded across her breasts, the other rests by her side. It is a work of a severe beauty, which had as yet never been equalled in English sculpture, but it is curiously unemotional, given the great grief from which it came. It is a royal symbol, excluding personal feeling. The canopy above it has gone; the carvings on its arcaded front where the shields of her descent hang from trees are worn and indistinct; but its splendid protecting iron grille survives, and has well fulfilled its task, for the figure is unscarred and admirably preserved. The stone crosses have fared less well, but those at Hardingstone, Geddington and

44 The tomb of Henry II and his queen, Eleanor of Aquitaine, at Fontevrault

45, 46 When
Eleanor of Castile
died in 1290 at
Hardby,
Lincolnshire, her
husband Edward I
had the body
brought slowly to
London, marking its
stopping-places with
memorial crosses.
Right: the cross at
Hardingstone,
Northamptonshire.
Below: Eleanor's
tomb in
Westminster Abbey,
a masterpiece of the
sculptor William
Torel

Waltham still stand, each with three figures of the Queen, and showing in their arches and buttresses the coming of the second, Curvilinear, Gothic style.

Such royal observances ensured that others, on a scale befitting their rank, would follow the example. Chantries, as these endowments were called, were set up throughout the country. Pious founders of religious houses, hospitals, and almshouses, benefactors of cathedrals or parish churches, expected that intercession should be regularly made for their spiritual welfare both before and after death. Later, colleges were added to the list, and here, if Masses have been discontinued, the frequent mention of *fundator noster* in bidding prayers and graces has proved a very lasting commemoration. Some of these foundations were corporate rather than personal in their purpose. Archbishop Chichele in 1438 founded All Souls College for the offering of prayers for the souls of Henry V, King of England and France; of Thomas, Duke of Clarence; and of other nobles and faithful subjects who died in the French wars, and the statutes stressed the obligation of prayer on his 'poor and indigent scholars' over that of study. Above the doorway a relief showed the Resurrection of the Dead at the Last Day, or so it is interpreted in the restored version made in 1826; it is possible that it may have been a rare example of souls in Purgatory. Chichele himself was buried in the choir of Canterbury Cathedral and to this day the College cares for the upkeep of the tomb.

Confraternities banded together to ensure their spiritual welfare. The Guild of the Holy Cross was already in existence at Stratford-upon-Avon by 1269, and today its group of buildings provides a wonderfully complete reminder of medieval activities. It employed chaplains, usually four in number, to say Masses for the souls of its members, living or dead, both in the Guild chapel and at altars supported by the Guild in the parish church. That church itself was served by a collegiate body, founded by John de Stratford, Bishop of Winchester, who added to the church in 1331 a chapel of St Thomas the Martyr where Masses were to be celebrated for himself and his relatives. The Guild came to have many other functions – a school, almshouses, property-owning in the town, upkeep of the bridge over the Avon – but its prime commitment remained unchanged. Over the chancel arch of its chapel can still be seen the painting of the Doom.

47 Chantry chapels were endowed to provide permanent prayers for the dead man's soul. These two in Winchester Cathedral are of Bishops Waynflete and Beaufort

48, 49 William of Wykeham, one of the most notable bishops of Winchester and founder of Winchester College and New College, Oxford, died in 1404. At the foot of his alabaster effigy (*above*) sit three monks (*below*), interceding eternally for the repose of his soul

50 Another splendid chantry at Winchester is that of Bishop Fox (*above*), of the late fifteenth century

For smaller grants, obits could be obtained, that is, a Mass on the anniversary of the donor's death, either for a limited number of years or in perpetuity. The wealthier members of the community might endow a special priest for more frequent services, founding a chantry or trust for this purpose, and in some cases building a small canopied chapel round the tomb for the saying of the necessary offices. England is particularly rich in surviving examples and nowhere can they be better studied than in Winchester Cathedral.

48–50 Six bishops, Edington, Wykeham, Beaufort, Waynflete, Fox and Gardiner, a line stretching from 1345 to 1555, have their chantries here, vying with one another in their dignity, and illustrating stylistic changes over a period of two hundred years. Wykeham's chantry in one of the bays of the nave masks the archway in which it is set and thereby achieves a sense of soaring height compared with the open bays on either side; within lies the effigy and at his feet are three praying monks, sometimes more romantically inter-

47 preted as the master builders. Beaufort's chantry in the retrochoir, canopied by a forest of pinnacles, is Gothic art at its most elaborate.

47 Waynflete's is neighbour to it, more delicate and less domineering in design. The effigy, holding his heart between his folded hands, gazes up at an intricate canopy in the centre of which an angel displays his shield with the lilies that passed from him to the colleges of Eton and Magdalen. Henry V, whom Chichele had

50 commemorated at All Souls, had his own chantry chapel in Westminster Abbey, for which he left detailed instructions in his will with provision for 'every day three masses to be sungen in a fair chapel over his sepulchre'. The chapel is in the unusual form of a bridge spanning the ambulatory, and the sculpture includes many

50 heraldic devices, the scene of Henry's coronation, and the King mounted and arrayed for battle. It was the first royal chantry in the Abbey, but was to have a greater successor, the chapel built by Henry VII to replace the thirteenth-century Lady Chapel. It is the climax of Perpendicular Gothic, that peculiarly English style, but

52 the tomb that it enclosed was by the Florentine, Pietro Torrigiano, the first great Renaissance work in England. Splendid as Henry's memorial is, it lacks the clarity and directness of statement, the effortless sincerity, that can be found in the tomb-chapel ordered

43, 53–55 in his will by Richard Beauchamp, Earl of Warwick, who died in 1439: 'A noble knight as was well proved in his joustying at

Mantua, and at the General Council at Constance . . . and in the Wars of France.' 'I will that when it liketh to God that my soul depart out of this world, my body be entered within the Church Collegiate of Our Lady in Warwick, where I will, that in such a place as I have devised, which is known well, there be made a Chapel of our Lady well, fair and goodly built, within the middle of which Chapel I will, that my Tomb be made – Also I will that there be said every day, during the World, in the aforesaid Chapel, that (with the Grace of God) shall be thus new made, three masses whereof one every day of Our Lady God's Mother, with Note [or requiem] after, and as the Ordinal of Salisbury doth assign.' On a *Note 17* tomb-chest of alabaster, surrounded by bronze angels and cloaked *43, 55* mourners, lies the effigy of the Earl in plate-armour, his hands not *54* folded but slightly apart, his eyes fixed on the Virgin as she appears *53* carved on a panel in the eastern bay of the roof. The figure was cast by William Austen and probably designed by John Massingham, 'Kerver, Citizen of London', as he is described in the very detailed contract. The features are composed in broad smooth planes that echo those of the armour; the hands are carefully veined, perhaps on the advice of Roger Webbe, the Barber-Surgeon, whose name also appears in the contract. In its stylized simplification, the effigy has something of the certainty that came so easily to Florentine artists. Over it rises a metal framework, or hearse, upon which a black pall could be draped for the celebration of funeral Masses. The reredos of the chapel, now replaced, for it drew the fury of Puritan iconoclasts, contained the Annunciation, and in the east window, now only fragmentary, the Earl knelt before his patron saints. In the window arch is a series of carvings, fortunately well preserved, again of angels in their hierarchies, with God the Father at the centre of the arch; in the lowest niches are St Barbara, St Mary Magdalen, St Catherine and St Margaret. In the side windows was more stained glass, of which a choir of singing angels survives.

On the west wall the Last Judgement was painted by 'John Brentwood, Citizen and Steyner of London'. The chapel as a whole is a full and detailed scheme of the after-life, and the careful differentiation of the angelic hierarchies shows skilled theological knowledge. Even with its many losses, it remains one of the most satisfying renderings of fifteenth-century hopes of immortality.

51 The chantry of Henry V at Westminster Abbey comprises carved heraldic devices and scenes from the King's life, like this of his coronation

When in 1529 an Act was passed forbidding payment for Masses for the dead, the confiscation of the chantries was almost bound to follow. Parliament was, with some reluctance, considering an act to that effect at the time of Henry VIII's death. In 1547 their wealth was transferred to the Crown, and 'the vain opinion of purgatory' condemned. In all, 90 collegiate foundations, 110 hospitals and 2,374 guild and free chantries were dissolved. How many had already lapsed or been abandoned in good time it is impossible to say. One of the purposes of the confiscation, only somewhat partially carried out, was the foundation of grammar schools and the augmentation of the universities. This being so, the Oxford and Cambridge colleges, and those of Eton and Winchester were spared. Here and there lesser foundations also escaped, particularly almshouses, such as that at Ewelme, where in the church beside them prayers are still said for the founder, William de la Pole, Duke of Suffolk.

52 The tomb of Henry VII and Elizabeth of York (*below*) marks the end of the Middle Ages in terms of artistic style, since it is the work of the Renaissance sculptor Pietro Torrigiano. In form, however, it continues the medieval convention and is surrounded by a traditional bronze grill made by an English smith

53, 54, 55 The Beauchamp chapel at Warwick is the best preserved of English medieval family chapels. *Left:* the head of Richard Beauchamp, Earl of Warwick, died 1439. *Above:* the point of the vault towards which his eyes are directed, the Virgin as Queen of Heaven. *Opposite:* the whole tomb still with the metal framework ('hearse') over which the pall was draped

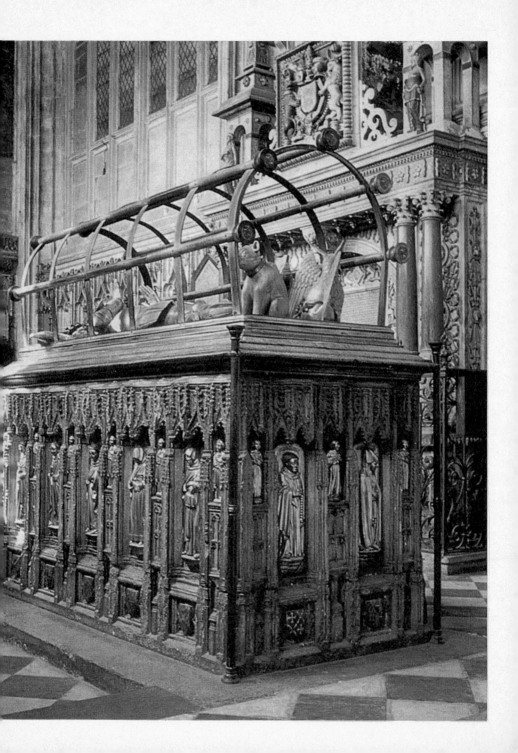

Chapter Four

Memorials to the Dead

Behind the religious dictates concerning salvation, memorials to the dead had other and more mundane purposes, and in particular the preservation of the deceased's repute and achievements. When in 1560 Elizabeth issued a royal proclamation against the defacing of monuments, it was to prevent the 'extinguishing of the honorable and good memory of sundry vertuous and noble persons deceased', and 'not to nourish any kinde of superstition'. This repeated the safeguarding clause in the act of 1550 against superstitious books and images, by which any 'image or picture set or graven upon any tomb in any church, chapel or churchyard only for a monument of any king, prince, nobleman or other dead person' was specifically excepted from destruction, thereby no doubt doing much to preserve our heritage of tomb sculpture. Here is the great breach in the uses of sepulchral exhortation. The 'phantasing vain opinions of purgatory and masses satisfactory to be done for them departed' had in England been condemned, and even prayers for the dead were viewed with suspicion. Tomb inscriptions no longer invoke orisons for the departed soul, but inscribe and praise mortal fame:

> Here lies within death's cold embrace
> A lovely darling youth
> Replete with every social grace
> Of Virtue and of Truth.

The glance is backward now, and does not search 'the undiscovered country'. Such commendations, the cult of fame and the precept of example, were of course fully accepted in the Middle Ages, even if subordinated to more speculative aims. The virtues of great men, William of Malmesbury had written in a dedicatory letter to his *Gesta Regum Anglorum*, were not only praiseworthy in themselves, but commendable in that they drew the admiration of others.

73

56 The bronze effigy of Bishop Evrard de Fouilloy (died 1222) in Amiens Cathedral includes censing angels, acolytes with candles and a dragon trampled underfoot

Tombs had always set out something of the deeds and functions of the man. The earliest medieval effigies, mainly ecclesiastical, show with some care the vestments that distinguish the office of 58 the deceased. The stone slab of a bishop in Exeter Cathedral, dating almost certainly from the last quarter of the twelfth century, is in very flat relief, set in a niche as though the transposition of a standing figure to a recumbent attitude. The bishop raises his right hand in blessing and holds his crozier with his left; he is shown, that is to say, in his most important living act; but under his feet is a dragon which he treads upon and transfixes with his crozier's point, and in the spandrels of the niche are two censing angels. The memorial is both symbolic of good triumphing over evil and also, through the angels, expresses a hope of salvation. There may well be in these episcopal effigies the further intention of preserving for their church the blessing of a notable incumbent of the office. In deeper relief and with much more lifelike reality, the funeral slab 56 of Bishop Evrard de Fouilloy (d. 1222) at Amiens shows the same gesture, the same trampled dragon and censing angels as the Exeter plaque, but adds two small acolytes holding candles. It is cast in bronze, a rare survival of the memorials in metal. Many of them, such as the plaque of Geoffrey of Anjou, were enamelled. This must have been the most splendid form of twelfth-century commemoration, though most vulnerable to the rapacity of the iconoclasts, whose rage in France, unlike England, was particularly directed against royal and aristocratic representations. Evrard de Fouilloy is particularly praised in an inscription as the founder of the new cathedral. Obligations towards benefactors is another and important element in the cult of the dead, and one which opened the churches as places of burial to lay patrons, whereas earlier convention had given something of a monopoly in such sepulture to ecclesiastics.

In the cathedral at Mainz, a wonderful repository of tomb 57 sculpture, Archbishop Siegfried III of Eppstein (d. 1249), a genial, complacent figure, crowns Heinrich of Raspe and William of Holland, neither of them ever securely seated on the Imperial throne. Though engaged in this activity and trampling upon a lion and dragon, the Archbishop still has a cushion behind his head and his staff lies on his body without any contact with the ground; the two emperors, much smaller figures, have consoles

74

57 The tomb of Siegfried III of Eppstein (died 1249), Archbishop of Mainz, ensured that the political power he wielded in life should not be forgotten after his death. With a somewhat awkward gesture he crowns two minor emperors who owed their thrones to his influence – Heinrich of Raspe and William of Holland. Beneath his feet, a lion and a dragon

58 *Below:* tomb of a Bishop of Exeter, perhaps Bartholomew (died 1184). He raises his right hand in blessing and with the other transfixes a dragon with his staff. Both tombs on this page display an uneasy compromise between the upright and the recumbent figure

59, 60 Two fifteenth-century tombs at Mainz show alternative conventions – the standing and lying positions: John of Nassau (*left*) in a canopied niche and Bernhard of Breydenbach (*right*) who, though recumbent, has open eyes

on which to stand. It is an uneasy compromise between recumbency and activity. By the middle of the fifteenth century Archbishop John of Nassau (d. 1439) stands firmly in a niche, and all reference to the prostration of death has gone. In the same cathedral, however, some sixty years later, Bernhard of Breydenbach, whose account of his travels to Jerusalem will always perpetuate his memory, lies with his head on a pillow, though framed in a niche, his alb falling in folds between his legs which are clearly shown beneath the thinness of the stuff, his hands crossed, a chalice upon his breast, realistic in every detail of his prone position, but even here the eyes are open. There was a strange reluctance in the North, as opposed to its full acceptance in Italy, to simulate the complete repose of death.

59

60

76

61 *Right:* William Longespée ('long sword') in Salisbury Cathedral (*c.* 1230–40) half turns his head, a move away from the strictly frontal pose

62, 63, 64 *Above:* Henry the Lion, Duke of Brunswick, next to his duchess, Matilda, holds a model of the Cathedral. Maria Vilalobos (*below*) in Lisbon Cathedral, reads a devotional book, while three small dogs gnaw bones at her feet. At Dorchester, Oxfordshire (*below right*), an unknown knight lies as if frozen in the act of drawing his sword

For the layman new motifs were needed. The effigy of William 61 Longespée in Salisbury Cathedral (*c.* 1230–40), the work of the skilled carvers concentrated in the West Country for the façade of Wells Cathedral, holds his shield, on which the heraldic device, originally coloured, must have been highly decorative, over his left side; instead of the frontal glance of the blessing bishops his head is half-turned, giving a new rhythm to the design. It was a rhythm that was to be infinitely developed. By the end of the thirteenth century, the unknown knight at Dorchester, fiercely 64 scowling, draws his sword from its sheath, while his limbs twist in agitation as though struggling to rise from the ground on which he lies. It is a marvellous design, curiously modern in its contrasts of solid and void; it is also a perpetuation of the active life, not an aspiration towards divine peace. There is much imagination in the search for suitable actions for these recumbent figures. At Fontevrault Eleanor of Aquitaine reads from an open book, or so late nineteenth- 44 century restorers interpreted a damaged remnant that in photographs seems less certainly identifiable; and in the cathedral at Lisbon Maria Vilalobos holds a book where the *Ave Maria* is 63 legibly inscribed, while round her feet three small dogs crunch the remains of a mangled chicken. At Brunswick, on a tomb made most probably about 1240, Henry the Lion holds a model of the 62 cathedral in which he is buried. Here, in the disturbed crinkles of the drapery, the strongly marked features, the pressure of the head upon the cushions, there is a new realism, a psychological interpretation of character if not an attempt at actual likeness. Beside

65, 66 Round the tomb of Louis de France
(*below*) moves a cortège of mourners in niches,
grieving for the lost heir of Louis IX. The effigy
itself (*right*) is among the masterpieces of
medieval art and is probably a realistic portrait

him his wife Matilda folds her hands in prayer, a gesture that was
gradually to supersede all others as that appropriate for effigies.
Almost contemporaneously with the work at Brunswick, Louis IX
of France showed on the tomb of his eldest son in the Cistercian
abbey of Royaumont (now in Saint-Denis) the young man gazing
upwards, one knee slightly raised as though alive, with his hands
joined in prayer. At his feet, instead of a dragon, is a small dog possibly heraldic but a companionable beast. Around the sarcophagus
is the funeral cortège, carrying the prince's bier, a cortège in which
the sons of Henry III of England assisted. Here is perpetuated the

65, 66

65

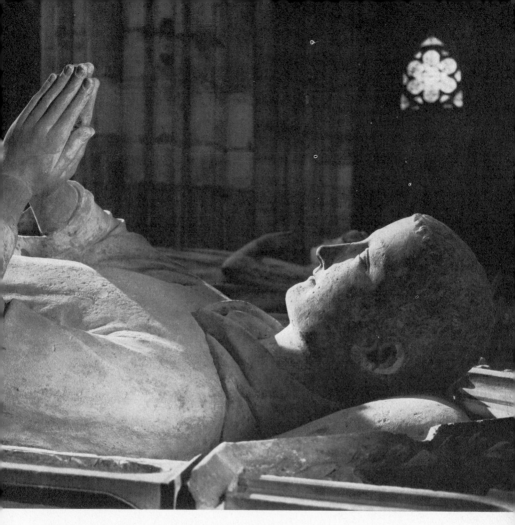

funeral pomp, the mourning for the lost heir, but above all it is the symbol of continuing prayer that is emphasized, the folded hands after the man himself has become inanimate, the permanent example stimulating the prayers of others for the welfare of his soul. A long chain of these praying figures lie on tombs throughout Christendom and survived the Reformation in many Northern countries, a severe and reticent contrast to the dramatic ecstasy and grandiose poses that prevailed with Baroque art. The Earl of Warwick's *53, 54* hands, not quite closed as his eyes gaze on the Virgin in glory, are as fine as any interpretation of this motif.

68 *Right:* a mourner, one of the daughters of the deceased, from the tomb of the comtesse de Joigny. Wearing a travelling dress, she gazes sadly down, one hand in the band of her cloak

69 *Above:* mourners
from the tomb of
Philippe le Hardi,
Duke of Burgundy.
The heavy drapery
is typical of the
school of Claus
Sluter

70 *Right:* eight
hooded figures,
heads bent, faces
hidden, carry the
body of Philippe
Pot, Grand
Seneschal of
Burgundy, to the
grave. This over-
life-size group is one
of the most
dramatic of all
funerary
monuments

84

The mourners round the tomb of the young Prince Louis were likewise to have many successors. They introduce a human touch, the sense of personal loss, the family bond. The tomb of the comtesse de Joigny at Saint-Jean at Joigny, dating from the end of the thirteenth century, has in the arcades of the sarcophagus her four children, dressed in the fashions of the time. One of the daughters, as she gazes mournfully downwards, links one hand through the band of her cloak and gathers its folds in with the other. On one end of the tomb is a curious carving of a young man clinging to the branches of a tree while two dragons gnaw at the foot of its trunk. It is a scene from the legend, very popular at the time with no awareness of its Eastern Buddhist source, of Barlaam and Joasaph, and here it symbolizes the insecurity of life and the heedlessness with which its dangers are constantly disregarded. It is a new element of fantasy in these carved meditations on mortality. There were to be many variants on these personal touches. At Bodenham in Herefordshire a lady has a child sheltering in the folds of her dress. The tomb at Elford in Staffordshire of the boy, John Stanley, shows him holding the tennis-ball with which in 1470 he was accidentally killed. At Lowick, Northamptonshire, Ralph Greene (d. 1417) and his wife touchingly hold hands; the contract for the

71 Instead of mourners, this knight's tomb at Howden, Yorkshire, is surrounded by minstrels

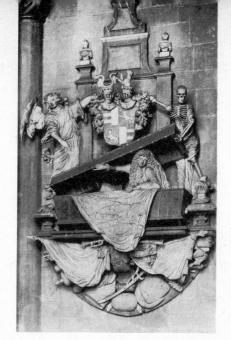

72 The display of secular pride, characteristic of late medieval tombs, reached a a climax in the seventeenth century. The tomb of Count Karl Adam von Lamberg, with its coat of arms, trophy and flags, is also in Mainz Cathedral

tomb, dated two years before Ralph's death, exists and specifically orders that his handclasp should be shown. At Howden in East Yorkshire the niches round the sarcophagus of a recumbent knight *71* are filled with minstrels. But these are relatively unusual details. The noble processions that surround the Warwick tomb and the great sepulchres of the dukes of Burgundy or the free-standing *69* figures that support the bier of Phillippe Pot are mourners, relatives *70* and retainers, not individually differentiated in their cloaks and hoods, but elements in a panoply of grief and departing pomp, testimonies of family and status that with all the accompanying heraldic display establish the lineage and prestige of the defunct, ensuring, as it was phrased in Queen Elizabeth's proclamation, that 'the true understanding of divers Families in this Realme (who have descended of the bloud of the same persons deceased)' shall not be 'so darkened, as the true course of their inheritance may be hereafter interrupted'.

On the tomb of Count Karl Adam von Lamberg (d. 1689) in *72* Mainz Cathedral, a skeleton raises the lid of the coffin, from which the Count, fully periwigged, emerges. Above, an angel, aided by a skeleton, supports the knight's coat of arms: below is a trophy of flags and arms. Secularism could go no further.

73 The most elaborate of all funerary art was reserved for the shrines of saints. *Left*: the bronze shrine of St Sebaldus 1508–19, by Peter Vischer and his sons. Thoroughly Gothic in overall design, its smaller subsidiary figures often show classical influence. It is carried on snails, symbol of the Resurrection

74 *Right*: the Arca of St Dominic, in S. Domenico, Bologna, the work of several sculptors over a period of several centuries, has been much altered. Originally it resembled the shrine illustrated overleaf. Only the sarcophagus contains work by the school of Nicola Pisano. The Saint's body was placed in it in 1267

75 *Left*: the shrine of St Peter Martyr, in the Church of S. Eustorgio, Milan. Like that of St Dominic on the previous page, it contains vivid relief scenes of the Saint's life. The caryatids represent the virtues; the figures between the panels, Church Fathers

76 *Right*: the Arca of St Augustine, in Pavia Cathedral, 1350–62. Inside the arcade angelic figures hold the Saint's shroud. Above are again scenes from his life. In the niches at the bottom stand the Apostles

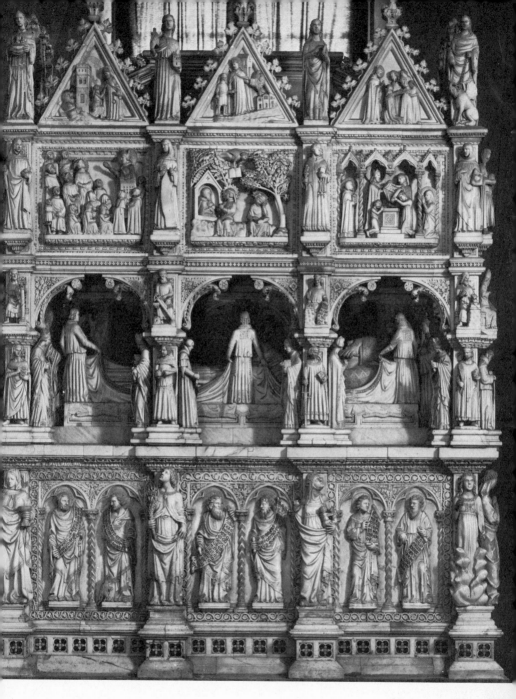

The finest craftsmanship and the most lavish expenditure were reserved for the shrines that contained relics of the saints. Their costly materials rendered them immediate objects of pillage in the English Reformation and the French Revolution. The 'degarnishing' of the shrine of St Thomas at Canterbury provided several cartloads of jewels and precious metals for Henry VIII. Germany
73 can boast Peter Vischer's superb shrine of St Sebaldus at Nuremberg, completed between 1508 and 1519, but it is in Italy that the most
74 elaborate shrines have survived, and of these the Arca of St Dominic at Bologna set an influential example. The work of Nicola Pisano and his school, it was composed of a sarcophagus supported on caryatids. The body of the Saint was transferred to it in 1267, by which date the sarcophagus must have been completed. In the relationship between the reliefs, corner and central figures, and supporting caryatids it is much influenced by the great Italian pulpits, but in the shrine a pinnacled canopy was probably always intended, though delays in carrying it out were such that the final figures came from the hand of the young Michelangelo, and Renaissance garlands take the place of Gothic ornament. Between 1335 and 1339 Giovanni di Balduccio created the shrine of St
75 Peter Martyr in the church of S. Eustorgio in Milan, where the sarcophagus has a sloping roof surmounted by a three-gabled tabernacle with the Virgin and Child between St Dominic and St Peter Martyr; the commission for the work specifies that it should be 'similar in every respect to that of our father St Dominic'. More elaborate, including a full-scale recumbent effigy, ninety-five
76 statuettes and fifty reliefs, is the Arca of St Augustine at Pavia, made by Lombard carvers probably between 1350 and 1362. These richly carved, free-standing monuments were not without their effect on
77 secular tombs. The tomb of Bernabò Visconti (d. 1385) is composed of a sarcophagus supported on pillars and surmounted by a large equestrian statue by Bonino da Campione, carved from one great block of marble and completed during Bernabò's lifetime. Bonino
80 also was responsible for the tomb of Cansignorio della Scala at Verona with its double tier of pinnacled niches, once more topped by an equestrian figure. The earliest, and certainly the most genial, of these mounted warriors was Cangrande della Scala, whose tomb

92

77 The tomb of Bernabò Visconti of Milan (died 1385) represents a new and unusual type, a sarcophagus surmounted by an equestrian statue

78 Ilaria del Caretto of Lucca is commemorated by one of the tenderest of early Renaissance tombs, by Jacopo della Quercia

was placed above the doorway of Sta Maria Antica in Verona, but in such a way that its upper storey and its rider were free-standing. Most Italian tombs are, unlike the shrines, placed against church walls, but they share with the shrines the Gothic gabled canopy, the sarcophagus and the supporting caryatids or pillars. The tomb of Robert of Anjou in Sta Chiara in Naples, partially destroyed in the Second World War, was one of the most lavish examples of the style, and included, as well as three representations of the king, figures of all the Neapolitan royal family. Free-standing chest tombs with recumbent effigies, normal north of the Alps, were rare in Italy; and the reassembled tomb of Ilaria del Caretto, that for Ruskin 'altered the course of my life', and whose effigy might pass for the diluted essence of all those figures that lie on Gothic tomb-chests, probably lacks a superstructure of a more Italian and, in all likelihood, distracting kind. Ilaria lies with her eyes closed in death. Beneath the horsemen of the Scaliger tombs lie effigies of the dead. Popes and cardinals sleep their last sleep soundly under Gothic as under Renaissance canopies: Robert of Naples, surrounded by virtues and relatives, enthroned in the highest niche, is still an old and wearied corpse. But if there is a quiet realism about the Italian approach, realism of a grimmer nature was to be found in the North in the later Middle Ages.

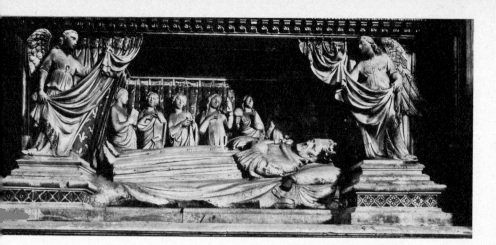

79 Robert of Anjou's tomb at Naples (*above*) belongs to a type popular in fourteenth-century Italy, with angels drawing a curtain revealing the dead King

80 *Right:* tombs of the Scaliger family, rulers of Verona in the later Middle Ages. The one in the foreground is of Mastino II, who died in 1351, that behind of Cansignorio della Scala, 1375

On one of the most beautiful Gothic tombs in England, that of the Duchess of Suffolk at Ewelme, the Duchess lies in prayer, her finely-drawn, aging features almost certainly a portrait; above is a choir of angels while on the sarcophagus other angels hold armorial shields; but below, through a tracery panel, can be seen a decomposing corpse, carved with infinite detail despite the obscurity of its position, stretched on its shroud, the long hair still falling from the skull. The Duchess died in 1475. She was a granddaughter of the poet Chaucer, and was twice married; her second husband, William de la Pole, the supposed lover of Margaret of Anjou, was murdered in 1450. She had had reason to think upon the mutabilities of life. More and more, the physical side of death was gripping men's imaginations. Beyond wars and violence, plague had always

82

81, 82 With the later fifteenth century came a concentration on the physical side of death. *Left:* detail from the tomb of Bishop Beckingham, Wells Cathedral. *Above:* tomb of the Duchess of Suffolk, at Ewelme. Beneath this stately effigy lies the grim cadaver

been the most dread adversary, but the Black Death of the fourteenth century had been unprecedented in the scale of mortality and an inescapable warning of how speedily men might be called to their account. 'Having to begin our treatise by recounting the extermination of the human race . . . my mind is stupefied as it applies itself to write the sentence that divine justice in its great pity sent on mankind, worthy by corruption of sin of the final judgment.' Thus wrote Matteo Villani when he undertook to continue the chronicle of his brother, dead of the plague in 1348. It was a new and abiding terror in men's minds, a judgment that implied their sinfulness and therefore the threat of Hell. When the Limbourg brothers painted in the early fifteenth century the *Très*

83 Riches Heures, they drew in much detail the scene of Pope Gregory the Great staying the plague in Rome, leading the procession through the town in 590, the year of his election to the papacy, when on the summit of Hadrian's mausoleum the Archangel Michael appeared, sheathing his sword in sign that the time of trial was over. Already in another work they, or painters of their school, had drawn the same scene, and closely following it, a procession of penitents, scourging themselves as they went, so that, by pain suffered willingly on earth, the rigours of Purgatory could be lessened.

> Since for the Death remeid is none
> Best is that we for Death disponę
> After our death that live may we
> *Timor Mortis conturbat me.*

Much earlier than Dunbar the tomb of the Black Prince at Canterbury, dead while the memory of the Black Death was still vivid in England, was inscribed with a metrical exhortation in French, thus Englished by John Weever:

> Such as thou art, sometime was I,
> Such as I am, such shalt thou be.
> I little thought on th'oure of death,
> So long as I enjoyed breath.
>
> But now a caitife poore am I,
> Deepe in the ground, lo here I lie,
> My beautie great is all quite gone,
> My flesh is wasted to the bone.

83 Pope Gregory the Great leads a procession to pray for the cessation of the plague: a fifteenth-century miniature. A monk and a child fall dying by the road

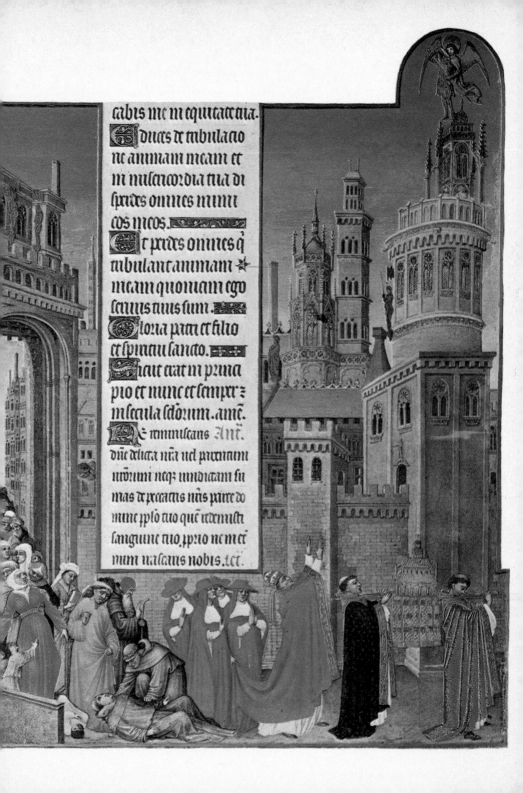

84 The contrast between earthly splendour and the grimness of death is emphasized in the tomb of Bishop Fleming in Lincoln Cathedral

85 *Below:* tomb of Cardinal Lagrange, died 1402. In his will he ordered that his body was to be 'boned', the skeleton buried at Avignon, the flesh at Amiens

86 Louis XII and his queen lie together in the abbey church of Saint-Denis, the stitches of the embalmers reproduced with gruesome realism

Beneath the recumbent effigies in their robes lie the skeletons, with little of the grisly details of decomposition spared, under the
84 elaborate tracery of Bishop Richard Fleming's chantry at Lincoln
81 (c. 1430), or that of Bishop Thomas Beckingham at Wells (1465), or, a hundred years later, on the tomb of William Parkhouse at Exeter. At Tewkesbury the tomb of John Wakeman (d. 1549), who adroitly succeeded in being the last Abbot of Tewkesbury and the first Bishop of Gloucester, shows a mouse, snakes and snails preying upon the corpse. In France there was the same lingering on decay. In the Museum at Laon is the sculptured cadaver of Guillaume de Harcigny (d. 1393), physician of Charles VI; in the Musée Calvet
85 at Avignon is that of Cardinal Jean de Lagrange (d. 1402), Bishop of Avignon and a great patron of the arts; another cardinal, Pierre d'Ailly (d. 1412), is similarly shown at Cambrai. Even in the magnificent elaboration of the tombs of Philibert-le-Beau and
87 Margaret of Austria at the church of Brou naked, half-shrouded bodies, though not yet marred by putrefaction, lie under the royally
86 clothed effigies. The corpses of Louis XII and Anne of Brittany, beneath their kneeling figures, have not yet decomposed, but along their bellies can be seen the stitches of the embalmers. As late as 1544 René de Châlons, mortally wounded, ordered that he should be shown on his tomb 'as he would be three years after his death' and Ligier Richier carved a standing skeleton, stretching up his hand, holding his heart, to Heaven. Here appetite for repulsion is almost sated, and by then this cult of the charnel house was on the wane, though the cadaver that lies beneath the effigy of Robert
88 Cecil, first Earl of Salisbury, in Maximilian Colt's stately Renaissance tomb at Hatfield, is as uncompromising as any of its predecessors. On the whole, however, the seventeenth century preferred the decency of shrouded figures to too accurate renderings of corruption.

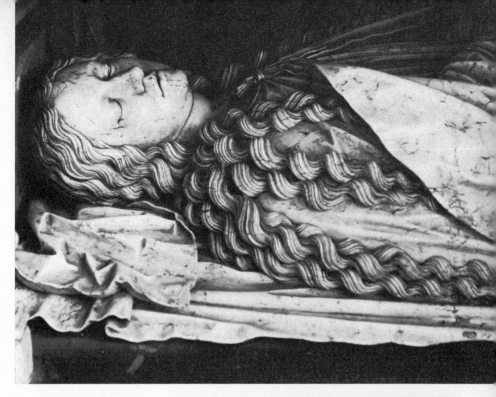

87 *Above:* detail from the tomb of Margaret of Austria at Brou, by Conrad Meit. The tomb follows the pattern of that of Bishop Fleming, the magnificently clothed figures above, the naked corpse below

88 The same convention continued into the seventeenth century. *Right:* the lower part of Maximilian Colt's monument to Sir Robert Cecil. The upper part is supported by kneeling figures of the virtues

89 The Dance of Death was a macabre idea which became strangely popular in fourteenth-century painting. The fresco at La Chaise-Dieu (*above*) is one of the best preserved

Dance of Death

One of the strangest manifestations of this morbid interest had been the Dance of Death. It originated in a late thirteenth-century poem, *Le Dit des trois morts et des trois vifs*, a subject carved on the façade of the Church of the Innocents in Paris at the orders of Jean de Berry, a man much concerned with death to judge by the elaborate arrangements for his own burial chapel. The same theme recurs on one of the pages of the *Très Riches Heures*. It spread rapidly throughout Europe, penetrating even Italy, where such macabre thoughts (the word 'macabre' itself first appeared in France *c.* 1376) were less congenial, and was painted, with many additional details, on the walls

90 of the Campo Santo in Pisa. In England it can still be seen on the walls of village churches, such as Widford in Oxfordshire; and in the pages of manuscripts such as the Lisle Psalter, as early as the first quarter of the fourteenth century. There is a naive but vigorous rendering of it, typical of the hold it had on popular art, in the church of Skiby in Denmark. The Dance of Death itself was sometimes performed as a masque, as for instance at Paris in 1422 and at Bruges in 1449, when men dressed as skeletons danced with figures representing the various grades of society; and a great wall painting of it decorated the cloister of the Holy Innocents in Paris, above rows of charnel houses where actual bones were exposed, a dismal décor which did not prevent these cloisters from being one of the popular rendezvous of Paris. The wall paintings at La

89 Chaise-Dieu and at Kermaria Nesquit in Brittany are the best surviving representations of the subject. Woodcuts gave even

90 Three young men out hunting come suddenly upon the three
corpses of – themselves! A detail from the fresco in the Campo Santo
at Pisa

wider circulation to the theme, such as those of Guyot Marchant published in 1485 or the far greater series by Holbein. Villon and other poets share in this obsession.

> *La mort le fait fremir, pallir,*
> *Le nez courber, les vaines tendre*
> *Le col enfler, la chair mollir*
> *Joinctes et nerfs croistre et estendre.*

('Death makes him shudder and grow pale, his nose curve, his veins stretch, his neck swell, his flesh soften, his joints and tendons grow and strain.')

It is a strange preoccupation with putrefaction. The Church had preached the transience of mortal things, but there was in the fifteenth century in northern Europe a morbid indulgence in disgust which answered some need now hard to understand. The earlier Middle Ages had their fill of the horrors of damnation, and gradually the image lost its potency. The mind must in the end have developed resistance to such gruesome forebodings, and if it was still too dangerous to question orthodox teaching, there must have been many who rejected its crudity and substituted for its detailed realism the less immediate awesomeness of the unknown. A more luxurious and sophisticated society concentrated on the physical corruption of their being. In a Book of Hours made for Mary of Burgundy and her husband, Maximilian, and probably only completed after her death in 1482, one page shows a terrible skeleton, his shroud falling from him, brandishing a spear and carrying a coffin. On another page three skeletons pursue a hunting party of a lady and two men, a version of *Les trois vifs*, but here surely with a reference to the hunting accident in which Mary lost her life. The scene has been copied in a later Book of Hours with opposite it an elaborate funeral procession, and in the borders skulls in niches, a motif also taken from the Master of Mary of Burgundy and one that was visible in actuality in many places such as the cloisters of the Innocents in Paris. In a painting in a Book of Hours of the liturgy in use at Bourges, from the second half of the fifteenth century, skulls are shown displayed in a gallery above a portico, in front of which death spears a young nobleman; below is depicted a graveyard.

South of the Alps there was, as has been said, less brooding on mortality; and even the Day of Judgment, until Signorelli's and

91 The hunters hunted . . . by death: a page from the Book of Hours of Mary of Burgundy, painted after her death in a hunting accident in 1482

92 'For the trumpet shall sound and the dead shall be raised': a detail from the west front of Orvieto Cathedral. In the upper section the blessed are clothed by angels

Michelangelo's frescoes, is handled with far less conviction than in the great tympana of north-west Europe. On the east end of the Arena chapel in Padua, Giotto's Hell, with its small, insect-like figures, has none of the solid reality that he gives to his procession of the elect. On the façade of Orvieto Cathedral the rising dead and the newly-clad blessed have a sensitive nobility that distracts the eye from the less skilful torments of the damned. A hundred years later, Fra Angelico (or some pupil working on his design) is much more entranced by the joys of his heavenly garden than awestruck by the various circles of Hell. There were of course popular movements and excesses in Italy as elsewhere, but the clear, clean sanity of Renaissance art is on the whole untroubled by the ferocity of northern nightmares. It is all the more striking, therefore, when we find in one of the great key pieces of *quattrocento* genius a direct example of Gothic moralizing. In Masaccio's fresco in Sta Maria Novella in Florence, God the Father supports the crucified Christ, between the Virgin and St John and two kneeling donors; behind him stretches the famous perspective of a chapel roof, the fullest realization hitherto achieved of the new scientific approach to representation; but below, painted most accurately, lies a skeleton in a tomb, with the inscription, *Io fu ga quel che voi siete e quel che son voi aco sarete* ('I was that which you are and what I am that will you be'). It is the very phrase of the Black Prince's tomb in Canterbury.

92

93

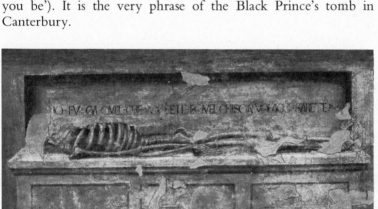

93 *Above:* Masaccio's famous fresco of the Trinity in Sta Maria Novella, Florence, includes this realistically painted skeleton at the base, which was only comparatively recently rediscovered

Burial was in the ground or in vaults. The body was wrapped in a shroud, knotted at head and feet. In many cases it was laid directly in the grave, but from an early date stone, wooden or lead chests were employed. In representations of the raising of Lazarus, where for a time there was some dispute with the Eastern traditions of emergence from a cave, the lid of the tomb-chest is generally being prised open by workmen, as in the well-known Chichester relief. The Gospels of Pembroke College, Cambridge, probably to be dated about 1125–35, shows Lazarus coming forth from a tomb 95 cut in the rock. The burial of Judas Maccabaeus from the Winchester Bible, where the shrouded corpse is being placed in a coffin, may be taken as an example of the common twelfth-century procedure, at least for men of note. In a splendid page from the York Psalter (c. 94 1170) in the Hunterian Library at Glasgow, the Virgin is shown completely swathed in grave-cloths, while the angels carrying her

94, 95 Two miniatures from twelfth-century English manuscripts show the shroud in which the body was wrapped. *Left:* the Virgin rising from her tomb, with angels unwinding the outer layer. *Right:* the burial of Judas Maccabaeus

96 As the coffin is borne to the requiem a gravedigger unearths bones from previous burials. A French fifteenth-century Book of Hours

97 *Above:* the corpse is washed, covered with a shroud and placed in a coffin. The widow sits apart

98 *Below:* Jacques Germain of Cluny, wrapped in his voluminous shroud

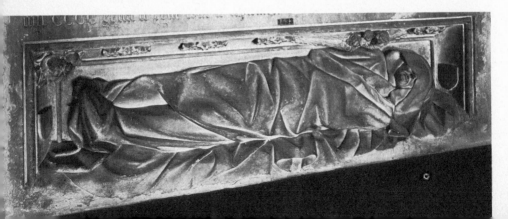

aloft from her stone tomb draw back the outer shroud as a means to support this corporeal assumption. Here was another theme, much debated from the second half of the twelfth century onwards, which provided many instances of burial illustration. From a later date a page from the Book of Hours of Philip the Good shows a more domestic scene, the interior of a bedchamber with the corpse 97 being swathed while the widow sits mourning. The tomb of Jacques 98 Germain (d. 1424), a bourgeois of Cluny, in the museum at Dijon shows him completely covered by a voluminous shroud.

Much importance was attached to the place of burial. Where land and status were so closely linked, it was natural to seek a grave in one's own territory, there to await the final resurrection. But this very desire caused a conflict. The corpses of great men dying far from their homes were sometimes dismembered, the flesh cleaned from the bones by boiling and the latter brought back to the native soil, while the other remains were buried at the place of death. Sometimes also the heart was buried separately from the body, as for instance was that of Aymer de Valence (d. 1261) in its shrine at Winchester. Here no doubt the wish to have some relic of a great man or benefactor played some part, but the theologians looked askance at this partition, which in an age so accustomed to visual representations of figures rising from their tombs raised obvious problems. Pope Boniface VIII felt it a sufficient abuse to require legislation against it. Embalming was also practised, but required skilled practitioners, and prolonged transits of the corpse could lead to ugly happenings. When Henry I of England died at Lyons-la-Forêt, near Rouen, in 1135, his entrails, brains and eyes were buried at Rouen and the body was embalmed in order to be taken to Reading, the abbey that Henry had founded 'for the salvation of his soul'. Such was the state of the body, however, when the embalming was carried out, that the surgeon died of an infection, 'the last of many', says the chronicler, 'whom Henry destroyed'. The body was carried to Caen, sewn in a bull's hide, and laid before the tomb of the Conqueror, where despite all precautions its noisome state was still apparent. It was well, Roger of Wendover remarks, that it was in the cold of winter that, some four weeks later, it finally reached Reading. In the margin of one manuscript is written: 'Note the vileness of human flesh. It gives cause for humility.'

113

Funeral Masses were occasions of great solemnity and are often shown on the appropriate pages of breviaries. The coffin covered by a great black cloth stood in the centre of the nave surrounded by mourners in black cloaks. Above it, for those of great estate, was an elaborate framework of wood or metal fitted with prickets for candles, which recalled the teeth of a harrow and so was known as the 'hearse'.

99, 100 Funeral Mass – the Office of the Dead – was moving and impressive, especially when private grief was combined with state pageantry. *Below:* the funeral of Charles VI in 1422. An effigy lies on the coffin. Members of the Parlement of Paris wear red instead of black. *Right:* funeral and burial scene from the *Grimani Breviary,* 1480–1520

When John of Gaunt, 'time-honoured Lancaster', died in 1399, he directed in his will that round his hearse there should be ten great candles for the Ten Commandments that he had broken, seven for the Seven Works of Mercy in which he had been negligent, seven for the Seven Deadly Sins, and five for the Five Wounds of Christ. Departure from this world and the passage to the next did indeed require forethought and precaution.

When in 1503 in Rhodes, Pierre d'Aubusson, the Grand Master, died and the coffin stood in the church of St John, there were on one side his vestments as a cardinal, on the other the hacked and battered armour he had worn in the defence of the island. On a Spanish tomb of the early fourteenth century from the monastery of Las Avellanas, now in the Cloisters, New York, the soul of the defunct, Armengol VII, Count of Urgel, is being carried aloft by angels, while on a long carved relief the funeral Mass is shown in progress. Funeral processions were also occasions of considerable display. In royal or episcopal funerals the corpse might be carried exposed in robes of office on a bier, but more often it was already in a coffin with a wax or wooden effigy lying upon the lid; more normally the coffin was draped in the pall, which varied from a plain black cloth, marked with a cross, to costly fabrics of velvet embroidered with cloth of gold. The pall used in commemoration services for Henry VII in the University Church is still preserved in the Ashmolean Museum at Oxford, and is a very splendid piece of work. A page in the Hours of Amadée de Saluces from the second half of the fifteenth century, nicely distinguishes the heedlessness of the choristers preceding the bier and the grief of the mourners following. Below, a gravedigger throws out bones with his spade, 'how the knave jowls them to the ground'. A strange and moving painting in a Book of Hours belonging to Philip the Fair while Archduke of Austria, illustrating the Vespers of the Dead, shows a naked corpse stretched on a tomb-chest in a church with mourners sitting below, a fantasy rather than an actual event. In two roundels on the border, skeletons seize a knight and a lady. It is curiously evocative of the emotions of the time.

99

96

101

101 In an unusual Book of Hours owned by Philip the Fair, the
corpse is shown like an effigy on his own tomb

102 'Into Thy hands, O Lord, I commend my spirit.' The dying man, in this page from the Rohan Book of Hours, speaks the Latin of the Psalms, God speaks in French

Chapter Five

The Art of Dying

In the business of dying it was all important to make a good end. On one of the bells in St Andrew's, Yetminster (Dorset), cast in 1608, is inscribed:

> I sound to bid the sick repent
> In hope of life when breath is spent.

Illuminations and woodcuts stressed the importance of deathbed repentance that, even at the last moment, might save the sinner from Hell and reduce the period of Purgatory. Numbed as the mind must have been by the too frequent harping on horrors, when death was at hand they must have taken on a new reality. On a splendid page of the Rohan Book of Hours (1418–25) a *102* naked corpse lies amongst skulls and bones; from his mouth comes a scroll: 'Into Thy hands, O Lord, I commend my spirit. You have redeemed me, O Lord, thou God of truth.' Above, a devil has seized his soul, but is being attacked by the Archangel Michael. From the clouds an immense figure of God looks down, bearing a sword, but answering: 'Do penance for thy sins, and thou shalt be with me in the judgment.' In a volume of French ascetic treatises in the Bavarian State Library in Munich an illustration to *La Science de bien Mourir* shows a singularly repulsive devil and an *103* angel struggling over a man's deathbed. A work known in many versions was the *Ars moriendi* to which was often added another treatise, the *Stimulus timoris Dei ad bene moriendum*. The Master known by the initials E. S. made for the *Ars moriendi* a series of engravings that were widely reproduced, and vividly showed contrasting scenes: on one page the devils surround the sick bed and eagerly point to scenes of fornication, murder and robbery; while on the opposite page St Peter with the cock, St Mary Magdalen, the penitent thief and the converted St Paul testify to the efficacy of repentance. Another pair of scenes show the sick

103, 104 The devil hovered near the bedside of the sick man, hoping to catch his soul if he died outside a state of grace. *Above left:* a deathbed scene from a French fifteenth-century *Art of Dying. Above right:* the sinner guilty of 'Impatience' kicks the doctor and overturns a table

104   man kicking the doctor and overturning a bedside table, while opposite are the patient martyrs and the suffering Christ. In the
105   *Grimani Breviary*, in the Marciana Library in Venice, there is a very detailed deathbed scene. Extreme Unction is being administered, while in the background two physicians hold a conclave and notaries draw up the will; in the curtains of the great bed an angel drives off a devil. Below is a vigorous rendering of the Trois Morts, skeletons fighting with three horsemen. 'Why dost thou not provide for thyself', wrote Thomas à Kempis, 'against the day of doom, when no man shall be excused nor defended by another, but every man's burden shall be enough for himself. Now thy labour is fruitful, thy weeping acceptable, thy mourning audible, thy suffering is satisfactory and purgatory. . . . Better it is to cut away and purge thy sins and thy vices here, than to reserve them to be purged in time coming. . . . Be now busy and sorrowing for thy sins, that thou mayest stand safe in the day of judgment with
Note 18   blissful men.'

120

105 *Right:* deathbed scene from the *Grimani Breviary*, described in the text above

106 A good life
made possible
(though it did not
guarantee) a pious
death, and for
practical purposes
had been reduced to
the seven principles
known as the
Works of Charity.
On this page are
shown
Admonishing the
sinner; Feeding the
hungry; Sheltering
the homeless; and
Clothing the naked

122

107 Visiting the sick; Visiting the prisoners; and Burying the dead. In the last picture the pious man dies and is taken up to Heaven. These miniatures are from a fifteenth-century Catalan version of *Breviari d'Amor*, a Provençal poem of about 1280

More crudely it was thought that death itself might be post-poned by good intentions. When the Empress Matilda lay griev-ously ill after the difficult birth of her son, the future Henry II, 'the prudent matron', we are told, 'distributed her treasures to widows, orphans and the poor and so escaped the peril of death'. But the wise man practised virtue throughout his life. An early fifteenth-century Catalan text, the *Breviari d'Amor*, has a page with
106, 107   scenes of the Works of Charity leading up to a very peaceful and pious deathbed, with the soul almost too complacently elevated by angels in a napkin.

Even when the last rites of the Church were not available, good intentions might do much. Joinville, in his *Life of St Louis*, has a touching story of how, when the crusading knights were prisoners of the Mamelukes and expecting death at any moment, they con-fessed themselves to one another. 'Messere Guy d'Ibelin, Constable of Cyprus, knelt down by my side and confessed himself beside me; and I said to him: "I absolve you, with such power as God has given me." But when I rose from there I could not remember
Note 19   a single thing he had said or recounted to me.' When Baldwin of Marash fell in an ill-judged attempt to regain Edessa, his con-fessor, Basil, wrote that though he had died unshriven, it was a martyr's death, and at the Last Day 'he will be crowned by God with the pious princes and the intrepid confessors of the faith, for such we know and believe to be the lot of those Christians
Note 20   who fall in war under the sword of the infidel'. This is not the immediate acceptance into Paradise that was claimed for some crusaders, for it is at the Judgment that his merits will receive their reward. Here it is a substitution for lack of confession before death. 'There pierced in the throat bloodying the plain, lost I sight and speech ended on the name of Mary. Truly shall I speak and you report it among the living, the angel of God took me, and one from hell cried "Wherefore robbest thou me, thou carriest away the eternal part of him for one little tear that takes him from me."' So spoke Buonconte of Montefeltro to Dante, among others who told of their late repentance, all of them asking for the prayers of their living friends: '*che qui per quei di là molto s'avanza* [for here, through those yonder, much advancement comes]'.

The Reformation brought a cleavage in the European view of mortality. Protestantism was eventually in some of its branches

124

to evolve theories of predestined damnation as terrifying as any medieval doom, but at first it weakened, with its denial of Purgatory, the certainties of the after-life, and its iconoclasm destroyed the visual exactitudes which had dismayed the Catholic world. The after-life never again was to be so generally accepted a concept; death ceased to be so clearly a stage in an inevitable progress. Shakespeare, son of a recusant father, was familiar with the Catholic doctrine. Hamlet's father returns from a purgatory where he is 'confined to fast in fires',

> Till the foul crimes done in my days of nature
> Are burnt and purged away.

The tale, did not 'the eternal blazon' forbid it, 'would harrow up thy soul, freeze thy young blood'. Shakespeare's audience clearly were well aware of these abolished theories, and in another speech, that of Claudio in *Measure for Measure*, he sets out the new uncertainties, the old beliefs still lingering on, and the fashionable preoccupation with decay:

> Ay, but to die, and go we know not where;
> To lie in cold obstruction and to rot;
> This sensible warm motion to become
> A kneaded clod; and the delighted spirit
> To bathe in fiery floods, or to reside
> In thrilling region of thick-ribbed ice;
> To be imprison'd in the viewless winds,
> And blown with restless violence round about
> The pendent world; or to be worse than worst
> Of those that lawless and incertain thought
> Imagine howling: 'tis too horrible.

The mouldering bodies carved below the tombs have their verbal equivalent in 'to lie in cold obstruction and to rot'; 'the fiery floods, and 'thick-ribbed ice' are the familiar extremes of medieval Purgatory, the suffering in which the soul delights because of its justice and the hope of redemption (Protestant commentators have made heavy going of the epithet 'delighted'), and 'worse than worst' the howling hopelessness of Hell. *Measure for Measure* is Shakespeare's most Catholic play; but the *via media* was in England already softening the impact. The age of epitaphs extolling a man's virtues and charities was at hand, a boastfulness which the Middle Ages, with all their pomp, would never have allowed. There was room too for more personal lamentation. On Roubiliac's monument of 1761 in Westminster Abbey to Lady Elizabeth Nightingale, a shrouded skeleton emerges from a vault, a successor to many late medieval fantasies, but, above, the sinister visitor is repelled by a gesture of the husband, who supports the dying lady. It is an affirmation of human affection in revolt against death, not a reminder of the dust to which we must all come. Medieval memorials are, with some few exceptions, lacking in tenderness, but they never lapse into sentimentality. They confront the predicament of mortality in varied ways, at times with an excessive panoply of display, but never without a basic resignation to a divine purpose, whose justice stood beyond question. Unfortunately for Christendom, this justice was given visual form in terms of Heaven and Hell, represented with such genius that they long dominated all thoughts of the life to come. Medieval Hell may have been at times a useful deterrent; it was certainly the grossest incident in the debasement of things spiritual to anthropomorphic crudities.

108 Fantasies of death multiplied in the plague years. This crowned corpse was added to an earlier manuscript about 1435. The tripartite banner is that of King René of Anjou and he may actually have painted the picture

Sequitur Officium Mortuorum

Notes on the Text

1 *Walter Daniel's Life of Ailred*, ed. F. M. Powicke, London 1950, p. 56.
2 William of Tyre, *A History of Deeds done beyond the Sea*, trs. E. A. Babcock and A. C. Krey, Columbia University Press 1943, II, p. 395.
3 *An Arab-Syrian Gentleman: Memoirs of Usāmah ibn-Munqidh*, trs. P. Hitti, Beirut 1964, p. 162.
4 E. A. Freeman, *History of the Norman Conquest*, Oxford 1875, III, pp. 497–98.
5 John Barbour, *The Bruce*, London 1790, II, p. 123.
6 Raymond of Aguilers, Ch. XXXVIII (*Recueil des Historiens des Croisades: Historiens occidentaux* III: trs. J. H. and L. M. Hill, *Memoirs of American Philosophical Society*, no. 71).
7 For *La Lumière as Lais* see Ch. V, Langlois, *La Vie Spirituelle en France au Moyen Age*, Paris 1928, pp. 66–121.
8 Fulcher of Chartres, ed. H. Hagenmeyer, Heidelberg 1913, I, Ch. III.
9 Migne, *Patrologia Latina*, CLXXXII, p. 591.
10 G. R. Owst, *Literature and Pulpit in Medieval England*, Oxford 1961, p. 299.
11 *Ibid.*, pp. 293, 294.
12 *Certain Sermons or Homilies Appointed to be read in Churches in the Time of Queen Elizabeth*, Society for Promoting Christian Knowledge, 1914, p. 94.
13 Peter of Branham, Balliol College MS. 208, 306, Q. 7, f. 284.
14 For the Dagobert tomb see M. Aubert, *La Sculpture français au moyen-âge*, Paris 1946, pp. 297–98.
15 J. H. Round, *Calendar of Documents preserved in France 918–1206*, 1899, no. 1101.
16 De Joinville, *History of St Louis*, trs. J. Hutton, London 1910, pp. 215–16.
17 For the Warwick tomb see P. B. Chatwin, 'The Decoration of the Beauchamp Chapel, Warwick', *Archaeologia*, LXXVII, 1928.
18 Thomas à Kempis, *The Imitation of Christ*, Book I, Ch. 24.
19 De Joinville, *History of St Louis*, trs. J. Hutton, London 1910, p. 97.
20 *Funeral Oration on Baldwin of Marash*, *Recueil des Historiens des Croisades, Documents Arméniens*, I, pp. 204–22.

109 Later tomb sculpture could still retain something of the drama and horror of the Middle Ages. This detail is from Roubiliac's monument to Lady Elizabeth Nightingale in Westminster Abbey, 1761

Select Bibliography

This book touches on many subjects, doctrinal, liturgical, artistic and historical and any attempt to provide full bibliographical reference would end in a lengthy document. For the doctrinal questions, such as the Last Judgment and Purgatory, the standard theological dictionaries, such as the *Catholic Encyclopedia* or the *Enciclopedia Cattolica*, can be consulted. The following brief list of books deals with the more general aspects of the subject.

CLARK, J. M., *The Dance of Death in the Middle Ages and the Renaissance*, 1950.

COOK, G. H., *Medieval Chantries and Chantry Chapels*, 1963.

DUBRUCK, E., *The Theme of Death in French Poetry of the Middle Ages and the Renaissance*, The Hague, 1964.

HUGHES, R., *Heaven and Hell in Western Art*, 1952.

KURTZ, L. P., *The Dance of Death and the Macabre Spirit in European Literature*, New York, 1934.

LANGLOIS, C. V., *La Vie Spirituelle en France du XIIe au milieu du XIVe siècle*, Paris, 1928.

OWST, G. R., *Literature and Pulpit in Medieval England*, 2nd ed., 1961.

PATCH, H., *The Other World according to descriptions in Medieval Literature*, Harvard University Press, 1950.

PANOFSKY, E., *Tomb Sculpture*, 1964.

List of Illustrations

132

detail from the Last Judgment tympanum of the centre portal, west front of Bourges Cathedral; 1270–80. From a cast. Photo Giraudon

24 The blessed, detail of the Last Judgment tympanum on the west portal of Saint-Urbain, Troyes; late thirteenth century. From a cast. Photo Giraudon

25 Resurrection of the Dead, detail of the lintel over the porch at Rampillon, Seine-et-Marne; early thirteenth century. Photo James Austin

26 Resurrection of the Dead, detail of the mosaic on the west wall of Torcello Cathedral; early twelfth century. Photo Alinari

27 St Michael raising souls to God, miniature from the *Shaftesbury Psalter*; English, mid-twelfth century. MS. Landsdowne 383 f. 168v. Courtesy the Trustees of the British Museum, London

28 Martyrdom of St Stephen, detail of a jamb on the west front of Saint-Trophîme, Arles; *c.* 1170–80. Photo Archives Photographiques

29 Tomb of Bishop Nigel (d. 1169); late twelfth century. Ely Cathedral. Photo F. H. Crossley

30 Death of Abbot Lambert of Saint-Bertin (at Saint-Omer, Pas-de-Calais), frontispiece

to a manuscript containing St Augustine's *Confessions*; French, twelfth century. MS. 46, f. 1v. Bibliothèque Publique, Boulogne. Photo Courtauld Institute

31 Soul of St Bertin carried up to God, panel from a polyptych attributed to Simon Marmion; *c.* 1459 or *c.* 1480. Courtesy the Trustees of the National Gallery, London. Photo John Webb

32 Demon on a capital at Sainte-Madeleine, Vézelay; *c.* 1130. Bildarchiv Foto Marburg

33 Detail of the stone effigy of François I de la Sarra; *c.* 1400. Chapel at La Sarraz, Vaud. Photo Gaston de Jongh

34 Second Coming, miniature from a Book of Hours; Flemish, end of the fifteenth century. MS. Add. 35313, f. 134v. Courtesy the Trustees of the British Museum, London

35 Dagobert rescued from the devil, detail of the tympanum of the monument to King Dagobert erected by St Louis; early twelfth century. Abbey church of Saint-Denis, Paris. Photo Raffaello Bencini and Liberto Perugi

36 Hell, painting on the west wall of the church of St Peter and St Paul, Chaldon, Surrey; *c.* 1200. Photo National Monuments Record

37 Detail of the *Coronation of the Virgin*, by Enguerrand Quarton; 1453–54. Made for the church of the Chartreuse du Val-de-Bénédiction at Ville-neuve-lès-Avignon, Vaucluse, now in the Hospice Civile. Photo Giraudon

38 Hell, detail of the centre panel of the Last Judgment altarpiece by Stefan Lochner; *c.* 1430–50. Wallraf-Richartz Museum, Cologne. Photo Rheinisches Bildarchiv

39 Abraham or God the Father with a soul in his bosom, detail of the canopy of the Percy tomb; *c.* 1342–45. Beverley Minster, Yorkshire. Photo Courtauld Institute

40 Dante, Virgil and the Falsifiers, detail of a drawing from Dante's *Inferno*, canto XXIX, by Botticelli; last decade of the fifteenth century. Kupferstichkabinett, Berlin-Dahlem

41 Hell and the mountain of Purgatory, detail of a fresco by Domenico di Michelino; 1465. Florence Cathedral. Photo Scala

42 Circles of torment from Dante's *Inferno*, detail of the fresco by Nardo di Cione; mid-fourteenth century. Strozzi Chapel, Sta Maria Novella, Florence. Photo Mansell-Alinari

43 Gilt copper figure of Warwick the Kingmaker, shown as a mourner on the tomb of his father-in-law, Richard Beauchamp, Earl of Warwick; *c.* 1450. Beauchamp Chapel, St Mary's, Warwick. Photo Peter Cannon-Brookes

44 Tomb of Eleanor of Aquitaine (d. 1204) and Henry II (d. 1189) in Fontevrault Abbey. Photo Archives Photographiques

45 Eleanor Cross at Hardingstone, Northamptonshire; 1291–92. Photo F. H. Crossley

46 Bronze effigy of Eleanor of Castile (d. 1290) by William Torel; *c.*1291–93. Westminster Abbey, London. Photo National Monuments Record

47 Chantry of Bishop William of Waynflete (d. 1470) and the chantry of Bishop Beaufort beyond (d. 1447), in the retrochoir of Winchester Cathedral, Hampshire; late fifteenth century. From Britton's *History and Antiquities of Winchester Cathedral*, 1817

48 Alabaster effigy (detail) of Bishop William of Wykeham (d. 1404); *c.* 1399–1403. Winchester Cathedral, Hampshire. Photo National Monuments Record

49 Three monks at the foot of the effigy of Bishop William of Wykeham; *c.*1399–1403. Winchester Cathedral, Hampshire. Photo Courtauld Institute

50 Chantry of Bishop Fox (d. 1528) in the retrochoir of Winchester Cathedral, Hampshire; late fifteenth century. Photo Courtauld Institute

51 Homage at the coronation of Henry V, detail from the north side of Henry V's chantry, Westminster Abbey, London; c. 1441–50. Photo A.F. Kersting

52 Tomb of Henry VII and Elizabeth of York, by Pietro Torrigiano; 1512. Henry VII's Chapel, Westminster Abbey, London. Photo National Monuments Record

53 Head of the gilt copper effigy of Richard Beauchamp, Earl of Warwick; c. 1450. Beauchamp Chapel, St Mary's, Warwick. Photo Peter Cannon-Brookes

54 The Virgin as Queen of Heaven, painting on the vault of the Beauchamp Chapel in St Mary's, Warwick; c. 1450. Photo Peter Cannon-Brookes

55 Tomb of Richard Beauchamp, Earl of Warwick; c. 1450. Beauchamp Chapel, St Mary's, Warwick. Photo Peter Cannon-Brookes

56 Bronze effigy of Bishop Evrard de Fouilloy (d. 1222); c. 1220. Amiens Cathedral. Photo Bildarchiv Foto Marburg

57 Tomb of Archbishop Siegfried III of Eppstein (d. 1249); c. 1250. Mainz Cathedral. Photo Bildarchiv Foto Marburg

58 Tomb slab of a bishop, perhaps Bartholomew (d. 1184); late twelfth century. Lady Chapel, Exeter Cathedral. Photo F.H. Crossley

59 Tomb of Archbishop John II of Nassau (d. 1439); mid-fifteenth century. Mainz Cathedral. Photo Bildarchiv Foto Marburg

60 Tomb of Bernhard of Breydenbach; c. 1497. Mainz Cathedral. Photo Bildarchiv Foto Marburg

61 Detail of the effigy of William Longespée (d. 1225); c. 1230–40. Salisbury Cathedral, Wiltshire. Photo Edwin Smith

62 Detail of the sandstone effigies of Henry the Lion, Duke of Brunswick, and Matilda; c. 1240. Brunswick Cathedral. Photo Bildarchiv Foto Marburg

63 Tomb of Maria Vilalobos; Lisbon Cathedral. Photo Mas

64 Stone effigy of a knight; c. 1295–1305. Dorchester Abbey, Oxfordshire. Photo F.H. Crossley

65 Stone tomb of Louis de France formerly in the Abbey of Royaumont; c. 1260. Abbey

of Saint-Denis, near Paris. Photo Courtauld Institute

Verona; fourteenth century. Photo Mansell-Anderson

81 Detail of the corpse on the tomb of Bishop Thomas Beckingham; 1465. Wells Cathedral, Somerset. Photo Courtauld Institute

82 Tomb with alabaster effigy of Alice de la Pole, Duchess of Suffolk; c. 1475. Parish church of Ewelme, Oxfordshire. Photo F. H. Crossley

83 Procession of St Gregory against the plague in Rome in 590; miniature from the *Très Riches Heures du duc de Berry* by the Limbourg brothers, 1488–90. MS. 65, f. 71v. Musée Condé, Chantilly

84 Effigy and corpse (below) on the tomb of Bishop Richard Fleming (d. 1431); c. 1430. Lincoln Cathedral. Photo Courtauld Institute

85 Corpse on the tomb of Jean, Cardinal de Lagrange, formerly in Avignon Cathedral; c. 1402. Musée Calvet, Avignon. Photo Archives Photographiques

86 Detail of the stone effigies of Louis XII and Anne of Brittany, inside their tomb; 1515–31. Abbey of Saint-Denis. Photo Pierre Jahan

87 Detail of the corpse of Margaret of Austria by Conrad Meit; first half of the sixteenth century. Abbey church, Brou,

Eure-et-Loir. Photo Archives Photographiques

88 Detail of the monument to Sir Robert Cecil, first Earl of Salisbury, by Maximilian Colt; seventeenth century. Hatfield House, Hertfordshire. Photo Courtauld Institute

89 Dance of Death, detail of wall-painting in the abbey church of La Chaise-Dieu, Haute Loire; c. 1460. Photo Archives Photographiques

90 Three Living and Three Dead with the hermit St Macarius, detail of a fresco of the Triumph of Death attributed to Francesco Traini; c. 1350. Campo Santo, Pisa. Photo Alinari

91 Hunting party pursued by skeletons, miniature from a Book of Hours of the Virgin (later copy of the *Hours of Mary of Burgundy*); Flemish, late fifteenth century. MS. Add. 35313, f. 158v. Courtesy the Trustees of the British Museum, London

92 The Blessed and the Damned, detail of relief on the façade of Orvieto Cathedral; c. 1310–30. Photo Mansell-Alinari

93 Skeleton in a tomb, detail of the Trinity, fresco by Masaccio in Sta Maria Novella, Florence; 1428. Photo Gabinetto Fotografico, Florence

94 Assumption of the Virgin,

detail of a miniature from a Psalter; English, *c.* 1175. MS. Hunter 229 f. 19v. Glasgow University Library, Hunterian Collection. Reproduced by permission of the University of Glasgow

95 Burial of Judas Maccabaeus, detail of a miniature (f. 350v.) from the *Winchester Bible*; English, second half of the twelfth century. Reproduced by permission of the Dean and Chapter, Winchester Cathedral. Photo Warburg Institute

96 Funeral procession and beginning of the Office of the Dead, miniature from a Book of Hours; French, *c.* 1460. MS. Add. 27697, f. 194. Courtesy the Trustees of the British Museum, London

97 Preparation of the corpse, miniature from the *Hours of Philip the Good*; Flemish, mid-fifteenth century. MS. 76. F. 2, f. 169. Koninklijke Bibliotheek, The Hague

98 Tomb of Jacques Germain, formerly in the Carmelite church in Dijon, Côte-d'Or; *c.* 1424. Musée de Dijon. Photo Archives Photographiques

99 Funeral procession of Charles VI, from the *Chroniques de Charles VII*; French, fifteenth century. MS fr. 2691, f. 11. Bibliothèque Nationale, Paris

100 Funeral with burial scene below, miniature from the *Grimani Breviary*, f. 450; Flemish, between 1480 and 1520. Biblioteca Marciana, Venice

101 Naked corpse and mourners, and in roundels skeletons seize a knight and a lady, miniature from the *Hours of Philip the Fair*; Flemish, late fifteenth century. MS Add. 17280. f. 271. Courtesy the Trustees of the British Museum, London

102 Dead man before God, miniature from the *Rohan Book of Hours*; French, early fifteenth century. MS. lat. 9471, f. 159. Bibliothèque Nationale, Paris

103 Deathbed scene, miniature from *La Science de bien Mourir*; French, fifteenth century. MS. Gall. 28, f. 5v. Bayerische Staatsbibliothek, Munich

104 Impatience (the fifth plate), woodcut from an *Ars moriendi* block-book with Latin text; southern Netherlands, *c.* 1450. British Museum, London

105 Deathbed scene with *danse macabre* below, miniature from the *Grimani Breviary* f. 449v; Flemish, between 1480 and 1520. Biblioteca Marciana, Venice

106, 107 Seven Works of Charity, and a pious death, miniature from a *Breviari d'Amor*; Catalan, early fifteenth century. MS. Yates Thompson 31, f. 109v. Courtesy the Trustees of

the British Museum, London

British Museum, London

Death comes to the printers and the booksellers: a woodcut from
La Grant Danse Macabre, published at Lyons in 1499

Index